USA –

Pleasure meeting You!

Cheers to A

Happy & Inspired

life.

:) Angela

A Charmed Journey

A Charmed Journey
An Inspired Guide to Personal Transformation

Angela@angelalenhardt.com

ISBN: 978-0-615-72605-2

1. SELF-HELP / Personal Growth / Happiness
2. SELF-HELP / Motivational & Inspirational

This book is published in the
United States of America.

A Charmed Journey

An Inspired Guide to Personal Transformation

Angela Dawn Lenhardt

Contents

Acknowledgments

Thanks, Mom! I had the best mom a girl could ask for. You taught me how to be and how not to be. To my brother, Jason, I couldn't have done it without you. Always offering your support and doing your best to keep me focused on my goals. And to my Dad, thanks for "showing up" and helping me fulfill my dreams.

I'm forever grateful for my friends, Joe and the late Noreen with providing me with a roof over my head and a shoulder to cry on. To Deb, Marek, Bennett and Gracie, thank you for listening to my stories and sharing your home with me. And a big thank you to Willy Mathes, my editor/writing coach—with your wisdom and expertise, this book did become my reality.

To my clients, supporting my emotionally and financially, believing in my talents and abilities. Thank you Dr. Teel from Mile Hi Church, Wayne Dyer, Neale Donald Walsh, Don Miguel Ruiz, Marianne Williamson, Doreen Virtue, Louise Hay and Carolyn Myss for relating valuable messages and sharing your knowledge in all aspects of life.

And, finally, thank you God, for listening, even on the days when I thought you weren't paying attention...To my angels and spirit guides, my animals and relationships, thanks for your patience. I know I may have caused a few gray hairs . . . but I wouldn't be the person I am today without your help. You have to admit, I *do* tend to keep life interesting, eh? ☺

Welcome Note

The lessons I have learned have been powerful and life-changing. I have seen Spirit work through me, my animals, my relationships and my clients in truly phenomenal ways. [Note to Reader: Throughout this book, I will be using the words, "God, Spirit, Source, higher power, the divine and divine intelligence" interchangeably. To me, they all refer to the same thing (and hopefully, this flexibility of language will engender a more inclusive, rather than exclusive appeal).] Miracles happen before our very eyes. As life unfolds, just when we think everything is under control, a "twist" arises in contrast to our plan . . . and life itself seems to await our reaction. If we remain focused and trust in the process, allowing the universe to work through us, we discover that our purpose is to be of service—as well as to live a glorious life. It's when we ignore our truth or doubt the magnificence of a higher power, we become detoured from achieving our greatest potential. How do we keep on our path? Keep asking for help, continue listening for guidance, and stay in alignment with who we are.

If you desire something different in life, now is the time to create an opportunity to make it happen. In today's world, most of us are faced with adversities every day, such as fear, a sense of not having enough, and stress. These factors *can* influence us to view the world as unsupportive, lacking and even hostile. This kind of outlook can only be a breeding ground for more fear and scarcity in the world, since like attracts like. At this moment, though, there seems to be a shift happening on our planet, as well as within each of us. This shift is our call to action to "show up" and take responsibility for all aspects of our behavior—to live with integrity, compassion, and respect for all. I believe we are all being held accountable for our thoughts, words and actions, and our lives are a reflection of such. The good news is, we are given plenty of opportunities to change our behavior—to open our hearts and live the life we were meant to live.

If now is the time for you to take a leap of faith, I encourage it. We don't get any of our days back, and we will never know what we are capable of achieving, if we don't try.

Through my trials and tribulations, I have maintained my faith in God and have seen the natural wonders of the Universe bestow their grace upon me. Developing and listening to my intuition has led me through my darkest moments; but my dedication to being happy and staying on purpose has been my primary inspiration.

I encourage you to keep the lamp of your faith lit, even when it seems there is no light at the end of the tunnel. How YOU live your life is a choice—a choice that only YOU are responsible for. Believe in never-ending possibilities and in the "magic" the universe holds . . . because it's always available.

You only have one life to live—design it, live it intentionally, and make it a good one. Anyone can have a mediocre life, but it takes the extraordinary to have an excellent one.

Namaste.

Introduction

Living a happy, passionate and soul-filled life has been my priority; but the journey has been anything but well-paved or uneventful . . . nonetheless, it *has* been quite charming (hence, this book's title). Yes, my road has been full of both magical and seemingly unfortunate ups and downs (all of which depend on your perception). There is always an element of curiosity within me that seems to keep my life interesting. Learning to stay in the flow of life and accepting "the way it is" has helped me to continue striving to attain greater heights and self-improvement. I have always known that my soul's purpose requires me to be of service to others, especially offering encouragement to those pursuing their dreams. However, I had no idea how my journey would need to take form in order to allow me to fulfill my purpose.

There came a time a couple of years ago when I realized the life I was living was exactly what I was *unconsciously* creating. From my living situation to the people in it, all of it was stemming from the thoughts that had been consuming my mind and many of the very words I had spoken. It was as though each thought or word was *becoming* my reality—and there was nothing "fun" or "happy" about it! I knew a higher power was asking me to show more consistent commitment to the life I'd intended for myself; and to own that it would only be through my decision to consciously create and be fully present in all situations that I would be able to inspire others to do the same. This challenging period forced me to grow up and take total responsibility for how I was "showing up" in this world, demonstrating faith and courage during times of hopelessness. The majority of my "learning experiences," back then, came about while running from one occupation to another, traveling from one continent to the next, trading in one relationship for a better one, and moving from home to home. Granted, this was an expensive and exhausting way to discover my true self; but these were choices I made while exploring life to find out who I am. It was no secret and it took only a short period of time before the satisfaction of eating out in extravagant restaurants, going on beachfront vacations, or buying new pairs of jeans wore off . . . and I was still left wondering what "it" was that seemed to be missing.

Fortunately for me, the Universe has provided me with plenty of opportunities to master myself, and in return, figure out what "it" is I've been seeking. I eventually came to see I had been yearning to understand where happiness really is and how to discover my purpose . . . and in the process, learn how my mind, body and spirit are intricately connected, and are actually *creating my life*.

Over many years of studying energy medicine, I began to understand how our bodies are composed of spiritual, emotional and physical energies, all working together to create our human experience. I became aware of how divinely guided we are; that is, *when* we take the time to open our hearts and listen to the messages that not only Spirit is relating to us, but what our bodies are also saying. It was difficult, but I finally grasped the importance of noticing how we recreate situations and magnetize specific kinds of people in our lives *until* we decide to change and adopt new ways of being. I came to recognize—with a lot of practice—that some habits are truly hard to break; but it has always been more uncomfortable for me *not* to try!

Looking back, I can find value out of every experience I've had. More often than not, though, maintaining grace during the experience was nearly impossible . . . but these days, I've come to realize it *can* be done!

A Charmed Journey was written for those who are discouraged about their path in life; those in need of motivation to believe there *is* a "higher power" actually guiding you; those finding it hard to trust in that "Universal Force;" those who want to live a life knowing *anything* is possible. This book is for those of you who are open-minded enough, and sufficiently willing, to simply surrender and remain focused on achieving your desires.

When the path appears grim and you feel overwhelmed with challenges, there is beauty in finding the strength to remain positive; there is a sort of grace or elegance when one chooses to surrender, while observing the synchronicity of events taking place that support your highest good. By reading this book and choosing to do your spiritual, emotional and physical "work" on yourself, *and* by using the gifts you have been blessed with, you may discover your sense of purpose in the process, building self-worth and self-confidence along the way. Mind you, these characteristics are not given simply by reading; but are earned through encountering obstacles and transforming them into opportunities for spiritual growth, seeing the lesson while in the midst of the experience (or afterwards, in reflection), and feeling a sense of accomplishment when it's done, i.e., learned.

There have been numerous times along my journey when I had lost my faith and felt abandoned to figure this life out on my own, seemingly doomed and destined to live my life on the streets. But then, out of the blue, I would hear words of inspiration or read something profound in a book, reinforcing my sense that Spirit is *always* working on my behalf, providing me with valuable insights, along with the support of generous people, so I could maintain the ability to stay in alignment with my purpose.

This book is comprised of three parts: my spiritual, emotional and physical interactions with the universe. These stories, I think you'll find, convey universal, down-to-earth, oftentimes funny and occasionally painful lessons, all of which had their influence in molding me into the person I am today. Granted, there was a point in the process of writing this book, when I questioned which stories I should include; but then, I realized I was inappropriately judging myself, and holding this or that story out of the book would sacrifice its authenticity. Therefore, you'll likely find the most out about me by reading through each story like it's a puzzle piece . . . each one intended to help make the most accurate picture possible of me *and* of the "messages" I want to share with you. Without a doubt, there is no replacement for devoting substantial time and energy into pursuing your dreams. However, one element many of us often forget is "giving back" to others . . . and that includes caring for animals and "Mother Earth." This sort of "selfless service" is how to truly discover your hidden talents, passions and the secret to your personal success.

From my experiences of consciously living a spiritually guided life, I have come to believe that each of us will be challenged to our breaking points, and brought to where our courage will be tested; but it is at these points and these places when and where we can choose to either stay committed to living the life we desire or to live by default. There isn't a right or a wrong way for living life. Like anything else, there are simply choices. However, I've found that the sooner we wake up, pay attention and be okay with who we are, *the happier we'll be*.

And So the Journey Begins...

I was raised on a small farm in Montana, where my brother and I taught ourselves how to make our own "fun," by climbing hay bales, riding dirt bikes and building forts . . . and I *loved* to run! I had plenty of practice to perfect my running abilities. My mother would pick my brother and me up from school, and often as we were driving home, I would get "mouthy" (as she would say) or repeat something I shouldn't have. Immediately I'd be told to get out of the car and run home. Although it was somewhat of an odd "punishment," nevertheless, Mom's discipline and my daily workouts paid off. I received track and cross-country scholarships, which paid for my college . . . and still to this day, I'm passionate about running.

Run! Run! Run! I have always been in a hurry, until now; when I've been forced to relax, slow down, and be patient. Not because I have *wanted* to, but because I have learned, the world does not "run" according to *my* time schedule.

I didn't grow up as a bible thumper, but I did grow up Catholic, going to church school on Wednesday's and mass on Sundays. My mother would come in my room, bright and early Sunday mornings, get me out of bed, and help me get ready. I would moan and groan about having to go, sometimes threatening to wear my pajamas; but my mother didn't care. Her response to me was: "God doesn't care what you look like, just as long as you show up." Interestingly, I have taken her words and applied them to my life today. It doesn't matter what I look like, just as long as I "show up." The truth is, some days aren't as productive as others: but I'm passionate about making a difference in this world, being happy, and living my dream.

Much of my character building came from various jobs. I've "done" or "been" all sorts of things, ranging from floral design to investment banking, interior designer, cocktail waitressing, hotel management, bartending in a strip joint –about that last one: I never once took off my clothes or appeared on stage—my mother threatened that if she had ever heard of me dancing, she would drag me off the platform by my hair. Later still, I went on to receive a certification in massage therapy, at which time, I began more formally integrating my intuitive insights.

These various positions have educated and prepared me for the professions I'm practicing today: as a consultant, speaker, and writer. I do practice what I preach, too. I try to lead a healthy lifestyle: whenever possible, I eat organic, non-processed or non-genetically modified foods; I drink plenty of water; I exercise; I make a conscious effort to be in a state of gratitude as often as possible; I PRAY A LOT . . . and yes, I occasionally eat chocolate, have fun, and laugh at myself often. But that doesn't imply I never fall off the beaten path; but when I do, I acknowledge myself for the way I am "being," allow myself a few days to wallow in my misery, and then I get back on the path I have chosen to travel.

Some would say, I have a "unique" connection with Spirit; or may even label "it" as psychic, clairvoyant, "a little out there," or "just weird enough to keep things interesting." But, I find it difficult to put myself into one category, so I tend to think of myself as "extra-ordinary" and simply living an inspired life.

It isn't like I'm Superwoman or I've climbed the side of a burning building to rescue any small children; but in the midst of my own "quandaries," I'm able to help others make sense of their own dilemmas, while I receive the guidance I need to keep moving forward with an optimistic attitude.

With that being said, the Universe and I have come to an agreement. If my purpose for being "here" is to be happy, live my dream and inspire others to do the same, especially during stressful moments in life, then I need "real" experiences relating to others, believing a higher power is indeed guiding each of us on our journey and is working for the greater good of all. In other words, I need to know that practicing this "spiritual stuff" helps make "dreams" a reality. Thus far, this is what my charmed journey has been about—discovering that dreams really do come true, and never underestimating the power of the Universe.

It was finals week during my last semester of college and I was living in my sorority house. I had spent countless hours staying up late and studying for my statistics exam (the class in which I had the least amount of interest and the toughest for me to comprehend). Passing this test was crucial for my graduation date. Because the nature of statistics consists of formulas and making calculations, we were allowed to use our book during the final. So, I stayed up late the night before, and prepared my book with all of the necessary notes and information. When I was finished, I placed the book on the coffee table in the middle of the living room floor, and went to bed. That following morning, I was on my way out the door and went to grab my book, but it was missing!

I started to pace the house, looking through desks, drawers, any place someone may have put it. I woke up everyone in the house, asking if anyone had seen it. No one had a clue, and now I was going to be late for class. Frantically, I ran to class and explained to my instructor the case of the disappearing book. (I'm sure this was *not* the first time he had heard a story of a "disappearing book;" regardless, I was telling the truth). Fortunately for me, he believed my story and allowed me to borrow a classmate's book to take my test during a class scheduled for later that afternoon.

I left the classroom and was more determined than ever to find my book. Again, I went back to the sorority house, and one more time, asked if anyone had seen it. "NO! NO! NO!" they all repeated. My next thought was to go to the bookstore. Because students were allowed to sell their books back at the end of each semester for a fraction of the cost, I was hopeful that is where I would find it. So, I walked on over and meandered through the store, stood in front of 400 returned statistics books, scanned the rows, and saw one that looked familiar. I pulled it out from the middle of the stack, opened it up and . . . *it was mine!* My notes were in the front of the cover to prove it! I took my book over to the cashier, and explained what had happened, and wanted to know who was responsible for the re-sale of my book.

When I had returned to the sorority house with my book in hand, I stood in front of the television set, not minding that I was interrupting *Days of Our Lives*. I looked at the sorority sister who stole, it, waiting. She looked at me, and didn't say a word. Suddenly, she jumped off the sofa, walked into her room, packed her bags, and moved out . . . right then and there!

Although it had been a hectic morning, I was still able to make it to the last scheduled hour to take my exam. Thank God for my instructor, who allotted me the extra time to complete the test. When I handed it in, I knew I had passed.

The Universe knew how badly I needed to pass my statistics exam in order to graduate from college. I had worked hard for four years, and I wasn't going to let a "missing book" stand in my way of my graduation date. In my mind, there was no question: the Universe intervened, guided me to my book, and I was able to fulfill that particular chapter in my life.

This was only the beginning of the journey I was unknowingly being prepared to embark on . . . but I had no idea it would lead me to the person who I am today. My conscious quest for happiness began about three years ago, when I lost most of my material possessions (due to financial difficulties), and then decided to sell my remaining items and live the gypsy/homeless life. Up until that point, I had believed that if I worked really hard to attain material possessions, then I would be happy. So I was working really hard, acquiring more and more stuff, but *not* understanding what the "need" was—that is, why I needed more stuff. Maybe losing all of my stuff was the Universe's idea of getting my attention, and it worked. I apparently had to be stripped of everything I once knew as my "comfort zone," and forced to rebuild my life from the ground up. But this time, I had at my disposal what I had learned over the years about how the Universe works on an energetic and emotional level. I was therefore able to use that knowledge to "cultivate" myself all over again *in a more conscious way*. Since everything I had was gone and my business had declined, I had plenty of time on my hands to sit and think about my soul's purpose and the next chapter in my life. Slowing down wasn't an option; it was a given. However, taking one day at a time, becoming fully present in the moment and getting okay with "what is" was the key to me recovering my inner peace *and* my accepting that balance was going to be my focus.

This is when I began to ask myself, *What is life all about?*

You see, it seems to me many of us have traveled (or are still) on the infamous "hamster wheel"—going a mile a minute, around and around. *Running to get where, though?* We run to work, we run to the grocery store, we run to meet up with a friend, we run home to take the dog for a run! What are we running for? I've come to understand we are all in the pursuit of happiness, aiming to fill the void in our hearts. But I think we're also, consciously or unconsciously, striving to find purpose in life. And discovering a purpose in life, in my eyes, has everything to do with living in a higher consciousness. Once I made a conscious choice to surrender having (what I erroneously believed to be) "complete control" over my life, and once I became more flexible in my thinking and able to appreciate the simple things, I slowly began transforming, like a butterfly, into the person I've always desired to be.

Certainly, happiness is different for each and every one of us. I can only write from my own experiences; but do yourself a favor and figure out what "it" is that you are seeking . . . *and choose to be it!*

Obstacles or Opportunities?

When life becomes challenging, it can become difficult to stay on your life path. One of the books that has been a significant aid to my getting beyond obstacles (and for my personal growth, in general), is Don Miguel Ruiz's *The Four Agreements*. Its central focus, I think, is "how to live your best life." One of the greatest lessons I've had to learn is one of the four major topics of his book: "Never take things personally." In my life, I have constantly gotten my feelings hurt by other people's words. The reality, however, is this: what they say about me isn't about me; and if it is about me, then it isn't any of their business, regardless of their desire to make it their business. As soon as I started using the principles from the *Four Agreements,* my world began to change.

Granted, at times, it was nearly impossible to always do my best. Doing my best was fairly easy around supportive people and in situations that were going my way; but my *real* growth came from dealing with the adversities that were my "triggers" in life . . . the ones that immediately provoked a negative reaction in me. In those instances, facing both the challenging situation or person *and* my reactive self simultaneously, I had to make a conscious choice to choose a different response, if I truly wanted a different result. Since I was relatively new at learning how to emotionally shift myself, I decided to take the advice of those who had "been there and done that" and who had persevered. My personal interpretation of Ruiz's "mantra" eventually emerged: *Don't waste precious time worrying about situations you can't control.* Expending energy concerning yourself with other people's perceptions, viewpoints and judgments (especially if these are aimed at you) will only take you further away from nurturing and realizing *your* dreams, and leave you feeling depleted and powerless.

Without a doubt, life *can* be difficult, demanding and seemingly "cold" to you. And sometimes, you *may* be asked to spend your valuable time and energy on doing things you have no (or little) desire to do. Big deal! Do it anyway! Embedded within the endeavor, you may discover a passion you never knew you had—

heck, you may even learn a thing or two! Even though it may not have been part of *your* plan, it may be part of a bigger picture, the Divine's plan for you. And at the end of the day, you can either choose to accept or resist the message the Universe is providing you. But from my personal experiences, the uncomfortable situations seem to have transformed my life the most. The hurdles that prove to be the toughest to overcome can be your greatest teachers in life, *if* you are willing to accept the challenge with an open mind and heart.

Though my years as working as a therapist, seeing clients on a daily basis, listening to their stories, I have found that the relationship between a person and his or her parents has a substantial impact on whether or not that person finds success and fulfillment in life. If the relationship with one's parent is hurtful or unsettling, it appears we seek relationships and environments to reflect those old patterns, so that we can (hopefully) mend those old wounds and get further along with our soul's growth. I believe that is why we are here, to evolve and grow as spiritual beings. So, it may well be that, in order to learn all that you can in this lifetime, you actually "chose" the parents you have. Sure, it's likely your parents don't see the world as you do, and have disappointed you or even hurt you, here or there. Some past event in your relationship with one or both of your parents may have even broken your heart. Do what you can to take such heartaches in stride; choose to rise up and heal, surrendering your needs about your past and getting on with the get on!

Choosing to remain a victim, or living in a constant state of resentment or fear, will only get you more of what you don't want. Your thinking and beliefs and actions are how you are "known" in the Universe, and the Universe will respond to your requests. What you appreciate will appreciate, and like attracts like. To get something different out of the Universe, you have to raise your vibration and shift your intention (and actions) to a higher consciousness. Make that higher consciousness your focus—by doing so, you'll be aligning your energy with the change you want to happen.

There are many ways to increase your vibration and become more aligned with your higher self. Methods I have used are meditation, prayer, sitting in nature, and eating healthy foods. But the most powerful way I know of is to be of service to others. When life is going well, it is easy to light up a room with a smile, keep your faith and stay on track; but the key is to maintain a high state of vibration as often as possible, even when "life sucks" and you have no clue about how "it" is going to work out. It is during the stressful times that your true self is revealed. If your habits of self-control and self-awareness are sufficiently developed—through consciously practicing such—then a sacred light will shine through what you do and say. The habits you demonstrate on a daily basis are the building blocks to a happy life, and are instrumental in your achieving any lasting fulfillment.

Being happy and living your life on purpose isn't for the faint of heart. The road may appear desolate, at times; but know you are never alone. Spirit is always there and available to guide you on your path, *if* you choose to listen to the messages that are being sent. Allowing yourself to seek quiet time throughout your day will give you clarity when seeking a direction . . . and will deepen your connection with Spirit.

Breaking the Cycle

Decide to be brave and step into your destiny. Albert Einstein once said, "A person who has never made a mistake never tried anything new." Isn't that the truth! I'm not sure if I can recall in my life that I made all of the "right" choices the first time. But that didn't stop from moving forward. Even though there were times when it was difficult for me to identify what it was that I most wanted to accomplish, I still did the little things each day that would move me in *a* direction, because being stagnant wouldn't get you anywhere! (At least I could then judge whether or not I needed to change direction or adjust something, based on the results I was getting.

You will never know what you are capable of achieving *until you get out of your comfort zone.* There is an art to picking yourself up, after your ego has been crushed or you've incurred some nasty bumps and bruises along the path you've chosen. Keep in mind that a mistake only happens once—after that, it becomes a choice.

There is definitely a learning curve when it comes to mastering yourself and enjoying the process along the way. Altering my behavior and changing my patterns has often been difficult. As a child growing up, we learn our behaviors and patterns from the people who support and teach us; but if they were "stuck" in their own emotional turmoil, chances are, they will pass those thoughts and actions on to you, consciously or unconsciously.

For example, my mother's way of handling her emotional stress was to drink alcohol and scream a lot. My father dealt with his issues by staying away from home for long stretches at a time. When he *did* come home, my mother would yell at him, and he would just sit and "check out" emotionally. So, in a sense, nothing was ever accomplished *and* neither of them got the results they really wanted. And, since I "took on" some of their patterns, I "did" a similar sort of routine and got similar results (i.e., no lasting fulfillment in my love relations), *until* I decided to do something different.

Many of these challenges were exhausting, but I was determined to get through it with a smile on my face and gain a better understanding of who I am and what this world is about. Taking down the walls I had up—due to my feeling like I needed to continuously be on the defensive—didn't happen overnight, *and* I'm still a work in progress. I realize, now, that when we can accept ourselves, we can accept others; when we judge others, we are judging ourselves; and when we try to control others, we are afraid of losing something or someone we have never owned in the first place.

According to many of the "spiritual" books I've read, our purpose in this world is to be of service to others, heal old wounds and live by following a Divinely guided path. *How do we do that?* The answers to understanding your path in life aren't "out there," and my hunch is no one will be able to give you *all* of the right answers, anyhow. Through my studies, I have found that opening our hearts to become one with our Source energy is our ultimate goal. There *will* come a day, I believe, when our journey on this earth has to come to an end, and we will continue on in another form . . . or maybe not. But just in case it's true, it seems to me we'd be wise to deepen our awareness of whatever it is that's responsible for our Being – which I like to call our Source (or Source energy). By doing so, my sense is we'll be led or guided most readily to knowing and Being who we really are.

One of my clients once told me, "Out of each death of me is born the best of me." I believe it! My old patterns had to die, so that I could recreate myself. I had to climb into my emotional closets and clean out the clutter. My desire to be truly happy was more important than carrying around the burdens I had been holding onto for years.

I have been on both sides of the spectrum of life, and my pendulum has swung from the highest of highs to the lowest of lows. If there is one thing that has gotten me through my life, it is my connection with Spirit, our Source, and keeping my faith. I enjoy living my life on the edge: taking a leap of faith and not knowing what the future holds, *but* trusting that I will always be provided for.

At one point, I didn't know "how" or "what" to change, until I started being conscious of my relationships. During that time, I started noticing how I was attracting people who were triggering my "old wounds," and they were causing emotional blow-ups within and with me. These eruptions didn't have much to do with the present situation, but they had been brewing for years and had finally reached their tipping point. One prime example was how I had held onto the old wounds of judging my father for his lack of ability to manage his money . . . and as a consequence, his "losing" our home. At the same time, my mother was dealing with her own sickness and emotional stress by confiding in the whiskey bottle. I was 15 years old when my father decided to leave my mother, brother and I and move in with another woman and her two children. It is safe enough to say, we all felt abandoned and hurt.

As the years went on, it became clear to me that these wounds only seemed to deepen with time. Not only did I lose my father, but at the same time, we were living on a farm that had been in our family for nearly 100 years. The financial stress that my father incurred during my parent's marriage was probably the most significant in their divorce. As a result, the farm went bankrupt and everything we had owned disappeared. As our world began to drastically change, we were forced off of our property, and my mother's drinking got to the point where she was no longer capable of taking care of my brother and me.

Given the stark situation, I had no other choice than to pack my brother's and my clothes and find a new place to live . . . in other words, look for a foster home. I'm not sure where I was able to find the courage to leave my mother and the only life I had known; but I knew, deep down inside, that my brother and I couldn't continue living in the chaotic environment we had grown accustomed to. I had no idea where to go, but I didn't care.

We got into my car and started going forward, completely on faith. My brother kept looking at me, asking where we were going . . . and I didn't have an answer. I guess I have always been blessed with an internal GPS, and luckily for us, it guided us to a safe haven.

I remember that, when we finally arrived in a town, I drove to a home owned by someone I assumed would care for us . . . because I knew the "town nurse" lived there. I got out of my car, walked up to her door and asked if my brother and I could spend the night. That "one night" turned into over a year; that is, we stayed there until my mother was able to get the treatment she needed and was healthy enough for my brother and I to move back in with her again.

There is power in recognizing your patterns, but it requires strength and courage to change them. I had to be honest with myself, and ask if the "story" I was repeating in my life was ""real" or if it was an "illusion." I came to realize, the longer you keep repeating the same story to yourself, the more convinced you are that it's "real" . . . *and* the more justified you become in your actions. I had to get to the point where I recognized the past is the past, the future is the future, and the only moment I have is the present. It finally occurred to me that I had been unconsciously sabotaging the present, the past *and* the future whenever I was living with self-limiting perceptions and judgmental resentments of others. I needed to change my way of thinking about both myself and others, and "show up" differently, if I expected something different out of life.

Who Doesn't Love Control?

My control issues weren't fun to admit to, either. I didn't know I was a "control freak," until someone drew my attention to it. One afternoon, I walked into my friend's home. I took one quick glance at his kitchen, went through the fridge and all of his cabinets, and told him about all the stuff he was doing wrong. Then I ventured through the rest of the house and told him how to rearrange his furniture. Granted, that date didn't last very long. I told myself I was only trying to be helpful with the knowledge I had to offer him. In my blindness, I couldn't understand why he wasn't welcoming my good advice. It didn't occur to me he wasn't asking for it and he was happy with the way his life was working. The bottom line? He didn't need my help. So I confided in one of my friends and asked for her advice. She gave me this analogy. She said, "Picture in your mind that you are standing in the middle of a hula hoop. And within the boundaries of the hula hoop is your business comprised of your thoughts, your actions and your behavior. You can micro-manage it, manipulate it or pretend it doesn't exist, because it is your life and you can choose what you want to do with it. But what is on the other side of the hula hoop is none of your business, and it is typically out of your control, anyway."

To conclude her counsel, my friend told me to stay out of other people's hula hoops, and if they want my opinion, they will ask.

Yes, since that time I have learned she was right: jumping into other people's hula hoops can only lead to conflict . . . *and* very likely, that person having hard feelings toward you. The more you are driven to push your opinion and thoughts into another person's life, the more resistant they feel about allowing you into their world. No one likes to be told what to do. If you want to attempt to get your point across to someone, it is good to keep in mind: how well the message is going to be received depends a lot on how well it is delivered (and that includes your sense of good timing).

Furthermore, when you feel the need to "influence"/control other people's lives, you are implying to them, you don't have confidence in their decision-

making abilities, *and* (even worse) you think you know "what's best for them." Now, while it may be you who actually knows what is "best for them" (given what you see going on in their lives), each person and every situation is unique . . . and unless they discover "the lesson" in this or that situation for themselves, they will very likely repeat it over and over, regardless of how well you "help" them with your advice.

We *all* may occasionally need guidance, support and honest advice; but it seems to me we have come here, at least in part, to learn many and obviously varying lessons. So, what gives anyone the right to take someone's lesson away from them? If you try *and* succeed in preventing a friend or a loved one from experiencing something, you may have just robbed them of an opportunity for them to learn a valuable karmic lesson. Moreover, it's likely the lesson will show up again in their lives, anyhow. Besides, their lesson is between them and Spirit, not between you and them.

To attain the skills I needed for my spiritual and emotional growth, I began taking meditation classes, reading self-help books, listening to CD's covering many topics, such as the akashic records, manifesting, the chakra system, and how to align with the natural laws of the Universe. I also began studying abroad, spending time in China and Thailand, living in monasteries, guest houses, and hostels, and investing in developing my own spiritual therapy, workshops and seminars. But to fully understand how all of this knowledge was benefiting me, the Universe had to make it "real," and present me with opportunities that tied all of my knowledge together. Even more, though, I believe I was then "tested" on it. Seriously! The Universe wanted me to do what?! *Use* this stuff?! Clearly, my taking notes in class just wasn't enough. I actually had to *apply* the tools I was learning to my life. *How was I going to do that?* I wondered. Ultimately, it came by way of my attracting relationships, animals and situations to me that revealed me to me!

I began to notice how I was recreating the same patterns, over and over, in my life. The only thing that was changing was the face attached to it; but underneath, the face was the same and was there in front of me, primarily, to show me a single, yet important recurring lesson. Interestingly, these seeming "obstacles" were actually transforming themselves into "opportunities" (or was it my own perception of them that was changing?), testing my boundaries and challenging me to show up differently than I had before – as the new and improved version of myself.

At the end of the day, my happiness was all about me. The more I began to understand who I was at the core of my being, I was able to get in touch with the "real" me. Not only was my mind beginning to change, but my body was, too. I started to lose weight, and began feeling more healthy and energized. I was amazed at how I started attracting supportive and optimistic people in my life, people who actually nurtured me and contributed to my growth. It should go without saying that the others, who were insecure with themselves and not showing they cared about growing personally or spiritually, were just disappearing from my life. As the saying goes, "Like energy attracts like energy. "

Gradually, the pieces of my puzzle continue coming together. I still don't know what the "big picture" looks like, but what I do know is, I am dedicated to living an extraordinary life. This, too, is clear to me: *The Universe is on our side when we co-create with it.* There truly are no limits to what we are capable of manifesting, when we stay in alignment with who we are, and we remain focused. One day, I saw this quote, written by Ruth Casey. Her words are very inspiring, and I remind myself of it often.

"It only takes one person to change your life . . . YOU."

That's for sure!

Part 1

The Spiritual Lessons

In my late teen and early adult years, I came from the philosophy that holds, you have to see it to believe it . . . but since then, I've changed my mind.

As I noted earlier, I use the words, "God, Spirit, Source, higher power, the Divine and Divine Intelligence" interchangeably. To me, it's all ONE—the source of the greater good. I will also refer to angels and spirit guides, which are known to me as spiritual helpers, and etheric or earthly "beings" who have influenced my path, those who are willing to show up at any time and in various forms.

At times, you may be able to see Spirit, and other times you might not be able to. Nevertheless, Spirit and these various spiritual beings are *always* there to assist you in finding answers, as well as offering divine guidance and support.

Extraordinary interactions I've had with Spirit, angels and spirit guides have led me to believe you are not alone on your journey. *Ever*. There is no "right" or "wrong" way to ask for help, either. There is no need to feel guilty because you are not "prayed up," and you only take the time to talk with Spirit when times are tough and you are in need. However, Spirit doesn't work like that --and it's a good thing it doesn't. The universe has *unconditional* love and doesn't judge; but people do. Spirit is always there to guide you on your path, but you have to be willing to ask for help and open your mind, as well as your heart, to receive it. I've come to understand that prayers are always heard, but just not always answered in ways you would have thought.

Early in my life, I had seen pictures of angels in books and listened to songs about them on the radio; but it didn't occur to me they were "real," until I needed clarification and a little rescuing. My interest with angels was piqued after this experience with my mother, which I'll recount below . . . and from then on, I began to study how angels can be so influential in our lives, if we simply choose to call upon them for guidance.

Dinner With the Angels

My mother believed in angels, and maybe that is why my name is Angela. Who knows, really—but from my first interaction or encounter with angels, through my mother's ability to see them, I was encouraged to believe.

It was the middle of the night and, like most people, I was sleeping. Having finished another semester in college, I was home for the Christmas holiday. Suddenly, I awoke to the smell of roast beef, potatoes and gravy! Immediately, I jumped out of bed, scooted down the stairs and demanded to know from my mom what was going on—for goodness sake, it was 2 o'clock in the morning! I found she was doing what she loved to do best: cooking. But given it was in the middle of the night, I wondered, *What is she thinking?! Why is she making dinner at this time?* I could only assume she was drunk.

I marched into the dining room and saw she had the table set for five. Crystal glasses, candles, and napkins folded in the shape of swans. Looking past the elegant setting, I shouted, “Mother! What are you doing?”

She replied, “Angie, please don’t be upset with me . . . Can’t you see, I’m making dinner for the angels.” This was just great! My mother had totally lost it!

“They don’t like it when you yell at me, so please keep your voice down,” she added.

Oh my God! Now, I *knew* she was crazy! She said, “Turn around and look at them.”

I turned around, only to see a pair of yellow and green Christmas bells hanging from the door. “There is no one here!” I yelled, as I yanked the bells off the door. Feeling so angry with her, I stood there and shredded the bells into tiny little pieces, such that cotton stuffing was flying everywhere. “Mother! There is no such thing as angels . . . and you’re *surely* not making dinner for them! The only angels standing behind me are these stupid bells! You need to clean all of this crap up and go to bed!”

I will never forget the look on her face. Empty, cold and heartbroken. I had just taken away a gift she was trying to share with me. She looked at me and said, “I’m sorry you don’t see them in the way I do.”

I stomped up the stairs, went back to bed and never spoke a word about angels or that experience again. That *was* the end of "the story," as far as I was concerned.

Years went by before I decided my mother was not as crazy as I once had thought, but it took for her to pass away before I began my spiritual awakening. While I was sitting at her funeral, unable to cry another tear, I had the thought to glance up and look at the ceiling. I witnessed a water drop fall from the ceiling and land on my knee. I'm sure, it is possible to say, the ceiling had a leak; but in my heart, I knew better. I felt my mother's presence was there and her love filled my heart. After the funeral, my brother and I were sitting in the car. I turned on the radio, and Sarah Mclachlan was singing, "In the Arms of an Angel." In that moment, I knew everything was going to be okay.

However, it took some time for me to really "get it." For awhile, after my mother's death, I felt lost and alone in life. Not knowing where to turn for guidance, and not having any friends who had been down a similar path before me, I needed some answers to this journey called "life."

One morning, I was reading the newspaper, and on the back page, I saw an advertisement for a psychic who supposedly could talk to people who'd passed away. I thought her profession seemed intriguing, so I made an appointment to go and talk with her. During my reading, I asked her, "Can you tell me whether or not my mom has any messages for me and what she thought my purpose was?" The psychic told me, "She says you are here to serve people and to help them heal." Interestingly enough, that had always been my mother's dream for me: to help people heal.

As it turns out, my mother had passed soon after my college graduation. Because the economy was booming and my degree was in business finance and management, the chances of me finding a job were likely; and even though her death grieved me, I was excited about my future. My first interview was with an investment firm, where I was hired on the spot and ready to take on the world. But it didn't take long for me to discover that answering telephones, sitting in front of a computer screen and crunching numbers was not the career for me. Within a month, I was looking for a new job . . . but what was I going to do? I had just spent thousands of dollars acquiring a degree that I had no desire to use!

I had always been interested in studying the body, but had no desire to go back to school to acquire a nursing degree. I also was lacking the dedication or the brain power to become a medical doctor; so, I opted for massage school. The year-long training program would allow me to receive a massage nearly every day, and I would learn how the muscles, bones and organs "communicate" with the therapist both physically, as well as energetically or spiritually.

Part of the curriculum for massage therapy was to take meditation classes. The concept of meditation was new to me, and it seemed *rather* odd to sit quietly, keep my spine straight and think about "nothingness." *How would this help me? I don't have time to meditate! I'm in a hurry to make money, find love and be happy! How could sitting and thinking about "nothing" move me in the direction I wanted to go?* But I did what I was told and learned to meditate, anyway.

During that initial instruction, I was taught there are numerous reasons why meditation is important for better health, stress reduction and an improved immune system. Personally, meditation has given me emotional stability. It has allowed me to temporarily get away from the chaos of the day, allowing me to calm my mind and be open to new possibilities, so as to make wiser choices and live a more peaceful life. I've also found meditation to be useful in listening to my inner wisdom and tapping into my intuition.

The more I learned about my intuition and the more I listened to my body, the more intrigued I became in developing a spiritual connection with the Universe. A friend of mine recommended I take a Reiki course and explained to me how this class was going to enhance my spiritual development. My first experience with Reiki consisted of receiving a treatment. Reiki is a spiritual practice developed in 1922 by a Japanese Buddhist, Mikao Usui. The Reiki practitioner I was treated by laid her hands on or above my body, and told me she was setting her intention on healing my whole body, spiritually, emotionally and physically, returning it to a state of homeostasis. She ended up doing a great job of it! I felt deeply relaxed, as though my body was vibrating at a higher frequency. I also felt I was being provided a deeper connection with "life source energy," and my intuitive skills seemed to be heightened drastically by the treatment.

When I say "drastically," I mean to a degree that I could have never imagined. Not all Reiki students will have this kind of phenomena or even the desire to experience this kind of awareness after a Reiki session or an "attunement" (an initiation that allows one to "do" Reiki). However, this was part of my soul's journey, and I was ready and willing to become more proficient in using my intuitive insights.

For those who may be interested in such, I'll briefly describe the experience I had on Sept 9, 2001, the day I received my first Reiki attunement. During this 5-hour class, I was taught Reiki symbols from a master Reiki instructor. She told me these sacred symbols were to be used with clients to intensify their healing session. She also mentioned that these symbols were now downloaded into my consciousness, and I was likely going to be experiencing a "shift" in my energy field. I had no idea, though, what kind of "energy shift" she was talking about, nor had I given much thought to what these "symbols" were suppose to do for me. All I knew was that when the class was over, I couldn't wait to get home. I was so sleepy, I practically needed toothpicks to keep my eyes open!

On my drive home, I began experiencing a debilitating headache. My vision became blurred and a nagging, piercing sound began ringing in my ears, reminding me of a "warning" signal in an emergency situation. I couldn't wait to get home, go to bed, and pull the covers over my eyes!

I was literally afraid, but I didn't know what I was afraid of. Rationally speaking, this emotion made no sense to me. I typically don't get headaches, have issues with my eyes, or feel anxious. But this was a different kind of sensation, a feeling that something "bad" was going to happen, like people were going to die, or maybe I was the one who was the one who was going to die. Like I said, I felt I just needed to stay in bed.

As the night progressed, however, the headache only seemed to get worse and didn't let up the following day, either. I was forced to lie in bed the entire following day and night!

On the morning of Sept 11, 2001, my alarm was set for 6:50 a.m. After I reached over to shut it off, I felt the need to turn the television on. The buzzing sound ringing in my ears instantly stopped and I couldn't believe my eyes. I was witnessing the attack on the World Trade Center and feeling the terror of the people who were there, running for their lives.

Lying in bed, I was trying to make sense of what was happening in the world, as well as the intuitive clarity and heightened awareness I was learning to tap into. I was feeling blessed, hopeless, and angry, all at the same time. There wasn't anything I could for those who were living in the horror and chaos, which I'd had the premonition about. I began to pray and hoped that this "nightmare" would soon be over. As we all know, now, the terrorism continues, although there have been "victories" against its spread and a greater sense of unity among those who seek to nurture a more peaceful world, too.

After finishing a series of Reiki classes and attunements, channeling life source energy for others, as well as for myself, became a part of my daily life.

After a year of massage school, I graduated and started my own massage therapy practice. I guess my business degree paid off after all—I've had my own massage business for over 13 years! But, in the short span of three years working as a massage therapist, my body started to experience many of its own aches and pains. Consequently, I learned how to compliment my practice by using my feet to massage my clients. I knew in my heart, though, this was only a temporary solution to the greater dilemma of "finding" my inner calling—the highest, most profound way I could be of service in this world.

Although, it was obvious that working in the corporate world could make me crazy, I was still pondering the idea of getting back to some corporate business profession. My thought was, *I'll just change my mind, force myself to like it and make the best out of the situation*, all the while knowing I was ignoring my inner voice that screamed, "This job is not for you!" Day after day, I resisted saying "yes" to the corporate gig, regardless of the retirement plans, paid vacations and yearly bonuses. But, even though I was still unclear on how I would make a switch in my career, I was committed to paying my bills through using my skills as a massage therapist.

I'm not sure if we *all* experience "ah-ha moments" or "wake up calls" in life, but I did. I knew I had been sitting on the fence of the "maybe's" and I needed to make a decision, one way or the other. I decided to use the meditation skills I had been taught to bring me clarity concerning my life's path toward a career using my abilities to communicate with and channel a higher intelligence. Well, my message came through loud and clear!

Wake Up!

One night, I had a dream about a client of mine, Sarah. In the dream, Sarah had cancer and, according to my dream, it was still a mystery to her. One thing more: somehow, in the dream, I was also the one responsible for relaying this message to her.

The following week, Sarah came into my office for her appointment. The thought of me telling her about my dream was on the tip of my tongue, but I chose not to repeat it. Although Sarah has an open mind and she would have found my dream interesting, I realized it was only a dream; and even though, it concerned potentially life-changing information, that information might or might not even be true. Therefore, I denied my "gut" feeling about mentioning my dream, and taking it another step further, I began asking Spirit to find her a different therapist.

Days later, a good friend of Sarah's called to tell me the news that I had already known. She had stage 4 cancer in her colon. After the conversation, I put down the phone and the feeling of guilt permeated throughout my body. I felt responsible for doubting a "gift" I had been given, because I was afraid of being wrong.

From that moment on, I decided I'd had enough of this so-called "healing profession" and using my intuition. I wanted a *real* job! I set an intention to have a heart-to-heart conversation with Spirit and discuss my future career plans.

That night, I went to bed and set my alarm clock for 6 a.m. Bright and early the next morning, the buzzer went off. As I was reaching over to hit the snooze button, I was suddenly pushed flat against the mattress, my arms plastered against my sides. I couldn't move or open my eyes, but I could talk.

I then heard someone walking through my front door, up the stairs, and straight over to me, where "it" stood at the foot of my bed. In a sleepy state of semi-shock, I said, "Who's there?"

I heard a voice. Although I wasn't sure if it was "real" or if it was in my head, the voice replied, "We are here because we understand that you want to renegotiate your contract."

Suddenly, I was frightened! Yes, Spirit was answering my request and we *were* having the heart-to-heart conversation I *had* requested; but I had no idea it would make the trip in person! I said, "Yes, I want to renegotiate my life's plan. I am tired of this 'so-called' gift and helping people. I want a *real* job."

"Great!" came the response. "You have the ability to change your agreement at any time, but are you willing to pay the consequences?"

I laid there, still unable to move my body or open my eyes. Images of how fortunate I'd been throughout my life began racing through my mind. I realized I had, indeed, experienced many challenges in my past, and currently was at a crossroads; but I also "saw" that I'd come through it all with flying colors. Spirit then asked again, "Are you willing to face the consequences?"

Because I was too afraid to ask what the consequences would be, I answered, "No, my purpose is to be of service by using the gifts I have been blessed with."

Spirit replied, "This is your one and only opportunity. Now, get up and show up in the best way you know how."

I didn't say a word. As Spirit turned around and ventured down the stairs, I heard the front door slam. It was gone! But, it wasn't until *then*, that I was able to finally roll over and shut my alarm clock off. Still unsure of what had just happened, and feeling it even more difficult for me to comprehend, I was temporarily afraid to tell anyone about this experience. However, I knew I had received the answer from Spirit I'd been seeking. Clearly, I did (and *do*, each moment) have a choice about how I wish to be of service in this world . . . *and* an option in deciding whether or not I wanted to use the gifts I had been given. Of course, saying "Yes," I intuitively knew, *would* be to my benefit.

Be the Light in the World

Just because life is difficult doesn't necessarily mean that we are on the wrong path. It is virtually impossible in life to live "solely on the surface," since we are *all* called, at some point or another, to go deeper within ourselves and "being" our purpose. At times we can have the misconception that if we are doing what we are meant to be doing to fulfill our soul's path that the answers should appear to be obvious and life ought to be joyful and harmonious, 24/7. However, I don't find this way of to be a healthy attitude to hold.

In fact, sometimes when life is the most difficult, it may be a blessing in disguise, forcing us to tune into and express the best of who we are. One of my instructors told me once, that when our hearts are broken, it can only mean they are more open to receive than they were before. Certainly, this perception requires me to trust that Spirit, God, the Universe, whatever one wishes to call it, loves me and is benevolently orchestrating things for my highest good, always and no matter what.

I believe that, at some time or another, we *all* will encounter a situation when we are unable to understand why the world is turning out the way it is. Such moments bring us to a place inside ourselves where we try to find the answer (or answers) to questions like, "Why do bad things happen to good people?" or "What can I do, by myself, to help stop all the violence in the world?" I don't think any of us have "*the answer*" to such questions, but regardless of the situation, we have to choose to stand in the presence of the divine and allow our light to shine. We must do what we can to help those who need support, especially those who are faced with major tragedies and struggling with such on their own. I try to go into such situations with a sense of knowing that, in any given situation, a greater good *will* manifest, the light of the divine *will* emerge, and a profound healing *is* about to take place.

With that being said, what *is* our purpose in life? I believe we all have a call to action to be "light beings," that is, to show up being the best person you can be, including supporting others on their journey.

To be one's best self requires you to free yourself from your emotional turmoil and to come to peace with yourself and others. Further, it requires you to love *who you are now*, and allow your light to illuminate the world . . . with love, faith, hope and peace. In this way, we will be making this world a better place for our having been in it.

From my personal experiences, I have tested Spirit numerous times and more than once, I doubted that a higher consciousness even existed. During these times, the world responded *immediately* to the emptiness I was feeling inside. I have to admit, it was a very cold, dark and lonely time in my life. Not only did I abandon everything that I once believed to be true, it was almost like Spirit agreed with me, and allowed my irrational thoughts and behaviors to consume me. And along with feeling that way, I attracted more of the same around me. I ended up in situations with more fearful, angry and manipulative people than I had never known existed. And that is because that is the life that I chose to see. As the old saying goes, "With light will come the dark." Still, we *can* choose to continue being the light when it is dark, and go on illuminating the path for others until they, too, find their strength.

Angels with Paws, Hooves and Claws

I began reflecting on what 'gift' I enjoyed giving most to others, and decided my communicative connection with animals had given me some of the greatest joy I had ever experienced. Not only can pets bring laughter in moments of loneliness, sorrow and stress, studies have shown that pets have a calming and therapeutic effect on a person's overall well-being and can help in lowering blood pressure, lessen anxiety, and influence a strong immune system—and I can't forget to mention, that animals can be great date magnets. If my animals didn't like the person whom I was spending my time with, or vice versa, chances are I wasn't going to, either.

The connection I experience with animals is apparently quite unique. It seems as though I communicate with them by observing their facial expressions, which then allows me to literally "hear" their thoughts. Because I've found the animals I've owned either on "death row," walking the streets or neglected by their owner, I've felt compelled to take matters into my own hands and adopt them into "my family." For this reason, I haven't found myself presented with the opportunity to pick one out for myself; somehow, *they choose me*.

These animals, though, have been with me through my marriage, numerous deaths of loved ones, my divorce, and both happy days and sad days, never leaving my side, giving me their undivided attention, until the day they died. Never once did I hear them complain about something they didn't have, unless, of course, they wanted a walk; and even then, truth be told, a walk would *always* benefit me as much as it did them.

Many "animal communicators" will say that animals are more grounded than humans, because they have four feet on the ground and humans only have two. Who knows if this is true? However, what I *do* know is, animals have an uncanny ability to forgive those who have said harsh words or used a "heavy" hand. It seems to me they desire only to please. In my view, animals are here to guide us, teach us, support us and love us. Animals never seem to question their owner's motives or even their own future. Their hope, as far as I can tell, is to have the safety of a home, combined with an atmosphere of compassion and kindness in which to live. In return, they naturally seem to extend unconditional love to us humans.

Three of the greatest lessons in life can be taught to us through our animals: trust, detachment, and unconditional love. Horses are here to teach us how to "trust;" cats teach us how to "detach;" and dogs teach us about "unconditional love. "

There are various reasons why a horse will buck. The factors supporting a horse's undesirable behavior range from being scared, hurt, poorly trained, or simply, they just don't like who's sitting on their back. Nevertheless, trust is essential for any rider, as well as for the horse, if both are to have a safe and happy experience. A horse needs to trust that whoever is riding won't lead him/her into a dangerous situation. Similarly, the rider needs to trust the horse won't buck, veer or do anything that could potentially cause serious harm. The bottom line is: it's a mutual relationship and partnership that is built upon the foundation of trust.

On the other hand, a cat can either take you or leave you. Sure, they appreciate the attention you give them; but contrary to dogs' and horses' natural impulse to please, cats are detached from your behavior.

Interestingly, though, cats are highly skilled hunters, as well as natural born healers. Regarding healing, many of them seem to have a calming and therapeutic effect, especially when it comes to helping us deal with emotional stress. For instance, whenever my cat detected I needed a "little extra" tender loving care, he wouldn't hesitate to sit on my lap or lay on my chest, using his paws to knead at me, giving me healing strokes that seemed to give me a sense of comfort, reassurance and peace.

As far as cats' natural instinct to hunt, think about this: when you're not home, your cat is very likely assuming you're out hunting! If they feel a close connection with you, though, they will hunt for you, whenever they get an opportunity to do so. There was a point in my life when I was going to school and working two jobs at the same time. I owned a cat, and keeping him indoors was not an option. He absolutely loved the outdoors, and would sit and howl like a wild animal if I made him stay inside. So when I would leave for work, I would crack the sliding glass door, which allowed him to come and go as he pleased. But, when I would come home, I would rush to the door, call his name, and there he would be, proudly standing on the back step, guarding his freshly caught prey. I couldn't help but feel horrible that he was catching small creatures, when he had plenty of cat food and tuna fish to munch on. However, I was told by an animal expert that it was my cat's way of showing me his appreciation. To him, it was all about the hunt.

The animal expert also mentioned I ought to acknowledge my cat for his outstanding hunting ability and thank him for bringing me a gift. So, I did start to praise him for his successful hunts . . . but I guess I wasn't convincing enough. He soon began catching bigger creatures! He had started out by catching small mice, decapitating them and setting them on the step. After my praise (and his recognition that mice were no longer a challenge for him), he began to catch squirrels. He then graduated on to rabbits, and finally he began catching huge black birds. He would rip their wings, then bring them into the house and set them in the middle of the living room floor. This is where I had to draw the line. I told him, "I appreciate all that you do for me, but I am capable of catching my *own* dinner. So, you can go back to being a loving cat, instead of a *wild* one!" To some degree, I think my lecture worked. Granted, he still hunted, but he no longer felt the need to bring his prey into the house.

What more is there to say about dogs and unconditional love? It is as though they go hand-in-hand. More than once, my dog jumped in between me and a rattlesnake, possibly saving my life. And when I crashed into a row of trash cans—because I was going too fast on my rollerblades—my dogs sat next to me, licking my wounds until I felt better (not once judging me for how reckless and irresponsible I was being). Or what about the time my dog followed me, swimming, out to the middle of a lake, while I was rescuing someone else's dog . . . and my dog helped me pull that dog to shore by grabbing its collar with his teeth? These are just a few of my experiences with my dogs, showing me the unconditional love they have, while expecting nothing in return.

And it's not just the love, but also the patience dogs are able to demonstrate and reflect back to us—both of which are traits that many of us could improve upon.

Being "only human," there have definitely been times when I became upset with my dog's behavior, prompting me to holler or scream or even throw a newspaper. Like many dog owners, I have spent thousands of dollars replacing tennis shoes, boots, cell phones, sofas, the legs of tables, mattresses, and even steering wheels, just because of my not picking up my things or shutting the door behind me, so they didn't have access to a room. Gradually, I figured it out! If you don't want them to get into it, then put it away! They are animals and have animal instincts: they like to chew stuff! But all my dogs were "patient" with me, as I eventually learned this simple lesson.

In summary, regarding our relations with dogs and their unconditional love, we get out of them whatever we put into them—including the time, energy and heartfelt love.

On more than one occasion, I have experienced the magnificence of how angels work though my animals and accompany them on their pathways. I wouldn't be a "believer," if I hadn't seen it for myself. Angels are, indeed, everywhere. And they often seem to show up on our path, just when we need them the most.

"Stud," the Wonder Cat!

At the time I adopted Stud, I was living in Idaho, sharing a house with three roommates, but I'd decided to move back to Montana. One of my roommates had gotten a six-toed, orange cat for his birthday. He didn't want the cat, though; therefore, he didn't take care of it. There was no way I could live in a house and watch an animal go without; so, I gave "Stud" his name and took on the responsibility of caring for him.

Things went along fine enough, for awhile; but when I decided to move out, I had a feeling that if I would have asked my friend if I could keep Stud, the answer would have been "no." To avoid the hassle, I moved out in the middle of the night . . . and not too surprisingly, Stud ended up in my car and on his way to living in Montana.

Driving over a mountain pass at 2 o'clock in the morning isn't one of the smartest choices I've ever made. Unfortunately, I ended up falling asleep at the wheel. The only part of the experience I can remember is miraculously waking up to Stud chewing on my ear, looking straight down the side of a cliff. Instinctively, I jerked the steering wheel, and somehow ended back up on the highway, pointed in the right direction. From that point on, for the rest of the drive, Stud sat on my shoulder or distracted me by jumping from seat to seat, keeping me alert and wide awake until we made it home.

Trusting in the Process

It was Halloween eve, the weather was below freezing in Sedalia, Colorado, and the rain had turned into ice. Bailey, my horse was in the corral; and at some point during the night, he had fallen and was unable to get up. The following morning, when I had gone out to feed him, I found him lying on his side, barely breathing. Bailey had gotten colic and it was necessary for him to be standing up again. My first instinct was to run to the house and call the vet, but then I sprinted to the neighbor's house, looking for someone to help me pull Bailey up off of the ground. Having no success, I returned to the barn and Bailey was on his last breaths. Helplessly, I lay on the ground next to him. We were both covered in mud from head to toe. All I could do was hold his head and pray that immediate help came quickly. But no one did, as I watched Bailey take his last breath. The kind spirit that had once shined so brightly in Bailey's eyes had disappeared and he was gone.

For me, losing Bailey was a traumatic experience and I decided to get out of the horse business for good. Surprisingly enough, Spirit had another plan for me—getting another horse and a lesson in trust. About a week after Bailey's death, a friend of mine called and mentioned a neighbor of hers was desperate to find her horse a different home, or else he was going to the "glue factory." I couldn't let that happen, so I was very quickly back in the horse business!

Trigger, a beautiful palomino who stood 16 hands high, was my new horse companion. It didn't take long for him and me to become the best of friends and deepen the trust in our relationship. On one Sunday afternoon in Littleton, Colorado, I really felt the need to get some exercise. I decided to go for a ride with Trigger. Because of my limited time that particular day, I decided we would both walk and I would guide Trigger with a lead rope. My goal was to reach an open space nearby where Trigger could graze and I could sit and relax. However, we both faced a challenge. Getting to the open space would require us to cross a busy highway and two lanes of traffic.

It turned out that getting to our destination wasn't the issue; it was the journey home that inevitably proved "interesting." When we arrived at our open field, I found a place to relax, and I slightly wrapped Trigger's lead around my wrist. I soon was enjoying the scenery and apparently not paying close enough attention to my surroundings. Suddenly, a deer leaped out of the bushes, startled Trigger, and he took off in a dead sprint for home. I jumped up and started running as fast as I could after my horse, but I knew my chances of catching him were slim to none.

Horrible thoughts of Trigger getting hit by a car began flooding my mind, and I knew it would be practically impossible for him to cross the highway without causing a disaster.

As I was racing down the trail to catch him, I watched as he crossed the first highway without hesitation. Amazingly, he got across it okay. But *then*, he started approaching the faster, dangerous lanes. I was running as fast as my legs would carry me, sweat was pouring down my face, and I was forced to trust that whatever was to happen was the way it was meant to be. My only hope was this: *If horses have angels, Trigger's would be paying attention.*

At that moment, I had officially lost sight of Trigger and then, out of the blue, there he was! I saw him standing still next to a woman whom I had never seen before. Now, the chances of a complete stranger catching a frantic horse seemed pretty well impossible, but who was I to question the help of some Divine intervention!

As I approached them, I thought to myself, *Who is this woman and how did she get here?* She graciously handed me Trigger's lead rope, and asked me if I had lost someone. My words were limited and all I could say was thank you, gushing to her how incredibly grateful I was. But I had to ask, "How did you catch him?"

She replied, "He seemed lost and knew where to go for help." I smiled, turned around, and we headed for home.

I had the feeling, if I had turned around, the woman would be gone. And, I was right! It was like she had vanished into thin air. I looked at Trigger and said, "You are one lucky horse."

When We Move On

From a young age, I've never been afraid of the thought of death. In fact, I've been intrigued by it. The questions of how we die or where do we go when we die piqued my curiosity soon after my mother passed. Therefore, to have some sense of clarity about the nature of death, I set an intention of seeking out some answers to my questions *and* putting myself in situations where I would find them.

Essa, my blue Persian cat, provided me with some clarity about death, during her own "transition process." She was a typical cat, one who loved to be pampered, groomed and carried around; but most of all, she loved eating baby food and tuna fish. They were, by far, her favorite treats.

I had owned Essa her entire life. When she was 14 years old, she started experiencing health problems and declined rapidly. During one afternoon, Essa took a turn for the worse and I immediately rushed her to the veterinarian emergency care. They gave her fluids and medication, but their advice for me was to take her home and hopefully she would snap out of it. I did what they told me to do, took her home, and put her on her bed. Because her breathing was shallow, I did everything I could think of to make her situation better. I put the humidifier next to her, used essential oils to freshen the air and washed her face with a warm cloth every hour; but nothing seemed to be working.

There came a point when Essa became incoherent, and I realized I was keeping her alive for my own sake. I was watching her suffer and couldn't take it anymore; so I called the veterinarian. The two of us scheduled to have her euthanized.

As the time was approaching her appointment, I wrapped her up in a blanket and told the dogs to tell her goodbye. Afterwards, Essa and I headed out the door. As I was carrying her out to the car, she leaped out of my arms and ran back to the house! Now, this was a cat who couldn't eat, walk or meow, but was sprinting back to the front porch! In that moment, I knew it wasn't up to me to decide her fate. Essa was going to die on her own terms and in her own way.

Essa survived the night. The next morning, I told myself, if her quality of life doesn't improve, I would have no other choice, but to make the decision for her.

That evening, I went out for dinner. On my drive home, I was dreading the thought of walking in the door and not knowing what I would find. But, Essa had found the strength to walk downstairs. However, she was lying on the cold cement floor. I sat next to her and began to cry hysterically. I could tell she was listening to me—her ears were twitching to the sound of my voice, and she was very inquisitive about every movement I made. I asked her what she needed from me, so she could "go."

I intuitively heard, "the rainbow bridge poem." So, I ran upstairs, dug through my closet and found the poem. After rushing down the stairs, I read it to her; but nothing happened—she was still alive. Now what! I was getting impatient with her. I could see that she was suffering and it was painful for me to watch. I said, "Essa, what else do you need from me in order to go?"

I then heard, "Psalm 23." So again, I ran upstairs, rummaged through the closet, and found my bible. (I don't think it had ever been opened; I may have even stolen it from a hotel!) I ran down to the basement, placed one hand on her back, while holding the bible with the other hand, and began reading the psalm to her.

When I had finished reading Psalm 23, I just sat there. The energy in the room was significantly different. It felt warm and tingly, almost magical. In that instant, my tears completely stopped, and I began to feel an overwhelming sense of peace. I sat quietly next to her and prayed. I felt heat coming from one side of the room. I glanced over my shoulder, and it was just like in the movies: a shiny white swirling cloud appeared—it was Spirit, coming to take her. I whispered in her ear, "Essa, they are here to get you; it's okay, you can go now."

I gently gave her a kiss, she took one last stretch, let out one more meow, and was gone. Just like that! I covered her with her blanket and let her lay there until the next morning.

I went to bed that night and couldn't believe what had just taken place. It was the confirmation I needed to know that we *do* have help when we die. I felt peaceful, grateful, and in awe about what I had just witnessed. I also was so grateful Essa had blessed me with her presence in my life.

We do have choices at the end of our journey. We can either choose to leave gracefully and effortlessly, or resist the inevitable, retaining fear of the unknown.

Two Big Hearts

There were countless times when my two faithful, amazing Labrador retrievers, Duke and Dakota, showed me the meaning of unconditional love; but there is one particular "event" I will never forget. Dakota had already passed away and Duke didn't have many days left, either. His hind legs no longer functioned and it was very difficult for him to walk. Although he didn't have much physical strength, Duke still weighed 100 pounds. Because his quality of life had been reduced to sitting under a tree, waiting for me to pull him around the block in his red wagon, I made my best effort to do whatever it took to make him happy.

One evening, Duke was in the house and needed to go outside to do "his business." It was pouring rain and the patio steps were wooden and slippery. Regardless, I picked him up and headed for the backyard. Just as I took the first step down the staircase, I tripped and Duke and I tumbled down an entire flight of steps and landed on our backs. The look on Duke's face was- . . . well, he turned towards me and I saw he had a smile on his face! It was as though he was saying, "Thanks! *That was fun!*" We both groaned, as we rolled over to get up. I picked him up, and we continued on with the task at hand.

There wasn't a thing I wouldn't have done for either of these dogs, or vice versa. They were always there for me and I showed them the same level of respect I would for a family member or loved one. It didn't matter if I had showered, what I was wearing, or if I was having a bad day—Duke and Dakota unconditionally gave me the gift of love and were always there for me when I needed them. Wouldn't that be something, if we all did that for each other?

Where is Home?

Since I have always wondered where "home" is, I decided, one day, to volunteer as a hospice worker, so as to put myself in a situation where patients were dying and some of them had the expectation of returning "home" someday. Throughout my experiences there, I found that the individuals who had only a number of hours or days to live were typically incredibly grateful for their lives and often wanted to make amends with family and friends. Many were also excited and ready to move on to another dimension, ready to leave their sick and tired physical bodies behind.

Certainly, there were those on the other side of the spectrum, as well. These were people who seemed to me to lack faith, or didn't have a belief system of any sort, relating to God, Spirit, or anything greater than themselves that would "be there for them." They often appeared scared by the unknown and resisted the inevitable. Their faces seemed sad and hardened. I suppose, on a deeper level, it had something to do with the openness of their heart. Either way, in hospice situations, time is limited . . . and they could either choose to accept the reality they were facing or resist it.

I can still remember Mrs. Johnson, she was one of my favorite hospice patients. Although she was very ill, she always had a smile on her face when I walked in her door. During one particular visit to her room, I could clearly see she was ready to go. Mrs. Johnson had her coat and hat on, her bags were packed, and she was sitting next to the bed. I said, "Mrs. Johnson, where are you going?"

She looked at me, like I was the one who was confused, and replied, "I'm getting ready to go home. They are waiting for me: God, my mother, my father, and all of my friends. I want to be sure I'm ready and I don't want to miss the bus."

I walked over to Mrs. Johnson, put my hand on top of hers, and said, "Don't worry about the bus. I'm sure they won't leave without you."

Mrs. Johnson looked relieved. She climbed back into her bed and closed her eyes. I stayed with her a few minutes, as she drifted off to sleep. I left her room and walked over to the cafeteria. As I was deciding on which patient to see next, a nurse came running down the hallway and made a beeline into Mrs. Johnson's room. I soon found out that my beloved Mrs. Johnson had passed and was on her way "home."

Part 2

The Emotional Lessons

Emotions: It's impossible to ignore them, and they are what they are.

Emotions often don't make sense, nor do they have to. But if we don't judge them as good or bad, there *can be* great power in acknowledging them, identifying the source of them, and setting them free. From my understanding, there are two basic emotions: love and fear . . . and all other emotions stem from these two.

When we live in a state of love, we trust and believe "everything" will work out for our highest good. Typically, our physical body also feels energized, we are able to stand in our truth, and we live passionately, regularly manifesting our desires. When we operate from a state of fear, our doubts, worries, and negative thoughts consume our minds, and the world becomes a scary place . . . and NOTHING works. We are out of the flow of life!

Toxic emotions, such as fear, guilt, resentments, worry, reside at a low vibration and can be detrimental to your health. The body is a wise vehicle. Its ability to manifest your emotions into your reality can have an overwhelming and lasting effect on your health. Over the years, as I've studied energy medicine and developed my own successful healing practice, I have watched many clients manifest serious health issues, such as pancreatic cancer, lung cancer, arthritis, knee problems, and debilitating migraine headaches, among others. What I have observed is that many, if not all, of these severe health issues have been due to their sustaining themselves—either consciously or unconsciously—in a constant state of emotional stress. When you begin to understand how the emotional body is connected to the physical body, and how each emotion carries the same vibration as the disease associated with it, you naturally begin to become more conscious in your thinking. You start to pay closer attention to what you are focusing your mind on, from one minute to the next. And that is wise; because as the ancient Indian teaching states: *What you put your attention on grows.*

In traditional Chinese medicine, I studied how the organs and emotions are associated and how they can affect the body. For example, disease of the liver is associated with anger, problems with the kidneys are related to fear, trouble with the pancreas is connected with worry, lung disorders are connected to sadness or grief, and issues with the heart are associated with a lack of joy. Applying the concepts of Chinese medicine and studying the work of Carolyn Myss and Louise Hay have made a significant impact in the way I think and my approach to the way I live my life. My studies of their work, in conjunction with my training in traditional Oriental medicine, have given me a different perspective on how I choose to react to my environment and the people in it, whenever I experience aches or pains. Because I choose to live in the city, surrounded by people and the hustle and bustle of life, there are numerous times when I *could* lose my patience. I've learned, though, that if the circumstance has nothing to do with me and I can't change it, then I simply *have* to let it go.

Realistically, I only have three choices when I find myself in an uncomfortable situation. I can accept it, get rid of it, or ignore it. Unfortunately, choosing the latter one will often create the most chaos in my body, if I'm choosing to ignore "it" and attempting to learn to "live with it." For example, I once was in a relationship in which I was constantly angry; but I wasn't conscious of the reasons why. I proceeded to bury my emotions, until one day, when they came to their boiling point. I should have recognized the signs my body had been giving me, but I ignored those, too! My eyes were always red, I would have severe pains in my neck, my breath smelled and tasted horrible, and to top it off, I had gained weight. My body was giving me all of the signs that signaled unhappiness, but I refused to acknowledge them or do anything about it.

Toxic thoughts and emotions are obvious to most everyone, *except* the person who is actually experiencing them. They linger over your head, and before you know it, a storm is born in your life, with all the dust and debris that accompany it. A visual image comes to mind: the *Charlie Brown* comic strip character, "Pig Pen," who is always surrounded by his own dust, dirt and grime. You can see it floating all around him, wherever he goes. This is a picture of *you*, if you have unresolved emotions lingering within your head or heart.

Have you ever been standing in a room and someone walks in with a "bad" attitude . . . or there is just something about them you can't quite put your finger on? Maybe it's the "toxic energy" they're emitting from having anger, sadness, fear or rage floating around inside of their heart or head. Another possibility is that they are triggering something inside of *you* that needs to be resolved. Whatever it is, toxic energy can affect the entire makeup of the room, as well as the people in it. Energy is contagious. A smile can light up a room, or a frown can destroy it; and many of us can spot a "fake" from a mile away.

But, I haven't always been aware of the subtleties of these matters. I've had to endure many aches and pains to get to where I am today. The following stories are some of the breakthrough moments I've had after years of dealing with the patterns and behaviors I've repeated. Finally, along came the "straw that broke the camel's back" (which you'll read about shortly) . . . and I had to change, if I ever was going to be happy.

Fear Hurts!

When I decided to study Thai massage in Chiang Mai, Thailand, I found myself immersed in a wonderful adventure and an eye-opening experience. I was fortunate to have the opportunity to meet friends whom I wouldn't have met otherwise, and I spent my weekends camping, hiking and backpacking, as well as studying massage, meditation and yoga.

That was my first trip to Thailand, short and sweet—and it inspired me to go back and learn more. But upon my return to Chiang Mai, my expectations were slightly higher. My plan was to attain an International Certification within the program, which would allow me to establish my own Thai massage school in the United States. After years of college and experiencing various occupations, I thought I finally knew what I wanted to do with my life . . . and I knew the rest would fall into place.

I went home and began planning for my next excursion to Chiang Mai. I registered for the extensive teacher training program and booked my flight. Because of the length of this program, I decided to live in a hostel, which would allow me to save some money, meet students from around the world, plus I would be immersed in the Thai culture.

To say the least, the trip began in quite an interesting and challenging way. Somewhere between the airports of San Francisco and Taiwan, I had lost my wallet; but fortunately, I'd decided to put an extra hundred bucks in my shoe, which was enough to get me by until I found a bank.

Once I had landed in Chiang Mai, I walked to the baggage claim area to retrieve my bags, only to watch every other passenger's bags circle around and around—except mine, which were nowhere to be found! Okay, by this point, I was beginning to lose my patience and my trip was becoming a little stressful! After an hour of sitting at baggage claim, wondering what to do next, I broke down in tears. Finally, one of the airport personnel walked up to me, gave me a Kleenex, and offered his assistance. He made some phone calls and discovered my bag didn't make it out of the San Francisco airport. He said not to worry, doing his best to reassure me it would show up in a couple of days!

Now, I was really stressed! What was I going to do? I had lost my money and I didn't have my suitcase. All I could think about was that I needed to get to the mall. I stood on the sidewalk, flagged down a tuk-tuk (a Thai version of a taxi) driver and requested he take me somewhere, anywhere!

My driver was both patient and kind, and understood my stress. (Although, looking back on the situation, it wasn't really that big a deal!) After he had taken me to the mall, where I purchased a few necessities, he then took me to my hostel.

As we parked, I couldn't help but notice the beautifully landscaped gardens and the flagstone path that led to the illuminated waterfall in the backyard. Eager to check in to my room, I was greeted at the registration desk and immediately handed my room key. Fresh floral arrangements and marble floors decorated the path to my room. Everything seemed to be going great . . . well, until I opened the door. I walked in three steps to find countless geckos scurrying up the cement walls, chasing each other and looking as if they were playing tag. And then, once I'd gotten over that, there was the bathroom. The place where I'd be "relieving myself" and prettying up consisted of a hole in the floor for a toilet and the end of a garden hose for a showerhead. These were *not* the living quarters displayed in the pictures on the internet *or* what I had anticipated. At that moment, I was unhappy, scared, cold, and hungry—once again, I sat down and cried!

Not only did it appear I was going to be forced to share my room with reptiles, but I had to use this one-of-a-kind sewer system, which was just enough to put me over the edge! I sat down on the bed, feeling miserable and alone, and began wondering who would ever find me if something happened. I also began to question my trip. Why did I feel the need to travel so far away from home? What was I trying to prove, when I could have attained a similar certification in the States? It didn't take me long to figure out the answer. My trip was about having a unique experience, studying a different culture, learning how to travel, and getting out of my own "little" world. But, most importantly, it was about my spiritual growth, and discovering "inner peace"—even when my world seemed to be consumed by unpredictable circumstances.

The thought kept swirling around in my head, *If I only had my luggage, my life would be better*. For whatever reason, I had bought into the illusion that my "stuff" would give me comfort. Obviously, "feeling safe and comfortable" was not part of the "Divine Plan." Apparently, Spirit was teaching me how to get "comfortable" in an "uncomfortable" situation, and seeing how I was going to react. Well, I cried non-stop, until I fell asleep.

Due to the change in time zones, my sleep schedule was completely erratic. I would sleep for an hour, wake up, fall asleep, and wake up again, until finally, I decided to get up and stay up. It was the middle of the night and I thought to myself, *I'm okay and everything is fine, since I'm still breathing.* In that moment, I had a positive premonition. My bag was at the hotel and waiting for me at the bottom of the stairs. I jumped out of bed, opened the door and saw it sitting at the bottom of the steps! Hallelujah! Life was good!

Grateful as I could be, I saw that things had started to fall into place. I had my luggage back and I was beginning to get comfortable with my living situation . . . even though I *was* still sharing it with the geckos!

I spent the following days getting acquainted with my route to and from school, and making some friends. I was even more excited by the fact that my life was finally headed in a particular direction. My career had always been my number one priority, and I now thought I had, at last, found my calling—or at least until I walked into the classroom.

On the first day of class, I got up early, ate breakfast and walked to school. When I placed one foot inside the door, my gut feeling was, *I don't want to be here*. Opening my own Thai massage school was, it seemed, *not* what I really wanted to do. *But, how could this have happened?* I wondered. Just moments before, I'd thought I had found my calling and had planned my entire life around it. So, what, now, out of the blue, I've changed my mind?! I had to come all this way to discover that "this" was not for me?! I guess what they say is true: sometimes, you can't know what you want, until you know what you don't want. And in my heart, I knew operating my own Thai massage school was not the career for me.

I felt, then, as if my life was blowing up in front of me, my dream was gone, and I couldn't do anything about it. Within moments, I started experiencing excruciating pain in my lower back, similar to a kidney infection I'd had in the past. By the end of class that day, I could barely walk and I was doubled over in pain.

I began trying to understand where my back pain was coming from; but instead of assuming I had pulled a muscle, my mind came up with its own conclusion about the pain. I thought, for sure, I had cancer or was dying of kidney failure. *My life is over,* I told myself.

I decided I needed to go to the hospital and have blood tests done. I phoned my tuk-tuk driver and, once again, hysterically explained to him my dilemma. I asked if he had the time to take me to the emergency room. Again, he was very patient with me, and immediately came to pick me up.

At the hospital, my doctor's name was Dr. Wong. He greeted me in the waiting room and took me over to the examining room. I was already starting to feel better, even though he hadn't done anything yet. As I took a seat on the hospital bed, he looked at me and asked, "What's wrong with you?"

I said, "You wouldn't believe it, but I think I'm dying."

He looked at me like I was somewhat crazy, then smiled, and said, "Okay, let's check it out." He had me lie down on the table, and then he tapped me on my forehead, on my heart and on my knee. He then told me to sit up. I was questioning his technique, since I felt as though I was on the brink of death and figured he should be doing something a little more sophisticated than tapping my body like it was a drum! Dr. Wong finally announced, "You are fine. You are healthy. You are just a crazy American. You come to Thailand and you have a big dream. All of you have a big house, a big car, lots of stuff and think very big. You think you have life all figured out. But life doesn't always work according to your plan. Don't be so stressed! Enjoy your life! Concentrate on happiness *and your pain will go away."* He gave me two Tylenol and told me to call him in the morning.

Whatever he did actually worked! By the next morning, my pain was gone and I had a huge smile on my face. Eventually, I realized my pain was, in fact, emotional, and indeed, it was causing my kidneys to react. But the key to releasing my emotional pain came when Dr. Wong addressed my fear and confronted me on my expectations of my trip to Thailand, as well as what I had expected from myself. That day, he was my voice of reason, and I mainly just needed to hear I was going to be "okay." Even though my life wasn't going according to my plan, I wasn't required to know what the "big picture" looks like, other than my enjoying the journey and being happy with "what is."

We Forgive, So We Can Move on With Our Lives

Carrying the burden of making others "pay" for how they treated you requires a lot of energy—energy that could and should be used to add to your life, instead of taking away from it. To forgive someone doesn't mean you let them off of the hook for what they have done. It means *you* are willing to move on, by releasing the anger that's holding you back, and allowing the Universe (or God or Spirit) to heal the past. Until you are ready to forgive the past, *you* are the one who still feels the pain. The person you're trying to hold accountable (for their actions) doesn't feel as you do about the situation, and there isn't anything you can do about it. The past is in the past, and reminding yourself of what happened in the past will only keep you stuck. Forgiveness isn't about the other person; it's about *you*. The negative energy you feel towards others will only take you further away from where you want to go; and what you want to have, I'd imagine, is happiness on the inside and out. So, put your attention on this approach to forgiveness, even for a day, and perhaps you'll see some amazing results, both within and without you.

And Clearly, Forgiveness Has to Do with Anger

Anger will hold you hostage by controlling your mind and, if it's not released or resolved, manifesting physical disease. To top it off, anger can cause wrinkles! And who wants wrinkles?! It seems very obvious to me: those who suppress their toxic energy lose their inner shine. My grandmother lived to be 104 years old, drank carrot juice every day, and had very few wrinkles. Her philosophy in life? "Let bygones be bygones, and never take it to the grave with you." To this day, her words are my constant reminder to carry on with *my* business, forgive and move on.

During my childhood years, my father wasn't often around. He was usually away on the weekends, or when he *was* in town, didn't come home until late at night. For this reason, while I was growing into a woman, I didn't have a lot of trust in men. I spent many years feeling angry towards my father. In order for me to have a successful relationship in my future, I had to mend our differences of the past.

As I grew older, the anger didn't go away, though. It just seemed to get worse. I was fortunate enough to attract trustworthy people into my life, but my insecurities would eventually end up sabotaging the relationship. I would unconsciously look for reasons why I couldn't trust the relationship, and ended up leaving it before it had a chance to begin.

I had no idea how influential my history with my father was, as far as determining the success of my personal relationships with men. Well, once again, Spirit was in charge, and led me into a relationship with someone who was wise, patient and compassionate enough for me to work through my old wounds with my father.

Ben was very honest and loving towards me, but there came a time when he was fed up with my insecurities. One day, he flat out told me I needed to heal my issues of trust and it needed to be done by forgiving my father. His exact words to me were, "You will *never* be happy in any relationship until you forgive your past."

I had no idea how trust and forgiveness were interrelated, but it was obvious that every relationship I was involved in fell apart due to my inability to trust. I wasn't sure about how I was supposed to approach a "healing" with my father, but Ben offered me a suggestion. He proposed that I sit down with my father and have a conversation with him, in which I would express how his behavior had made me feel while I was growing up as a young girl. I knew it was important for me to heal the part of me that didn't feel like she'd had a voice while growing up. And, hopefully, in return, I could break the cycle of sabotaging my relationships, and ultimately be on the right track regarding learning how to trust again.

Ben was committed to my success, which gave me both hope and courage. After setting it up as best as we could, he and I found ourselves on our way to Montana to work out one of the many "issues" I had with my father. I wanted to get this particular "conversation" with my father over with as soon as possible, so I could get on with my life. When we arrived in town, I phoned my father and set up a time for us to meet and have breakfast. Although, I wasn't quite sure if I was able to totally forgive him, I knew I needed to have this conversation. I kept reminding myself, *This is about me, not him.*

While were sitting at breakfast, my brain was going a hundred miles an hour, my palms were sweating, my heart was pounding, and my stomach was twisting and turning. Finally, I blurted out, "I forgive you, Dad, but I don't forget all the stress that you caused our family . . . but I'm working on it, and I realize that you did the best you could at that time in your life." I said it all in one breath and as fast as I could!

He looked at me and said, "That's great!"

After all those years of being angry, resentful and continually undermining my relationships, here I bare my soul to him and that was all he had to say?! In a split second, I realized, it didn't really matter what *he* said. *I* had needed to heal that part of "me" and gain the personal freedom of letting the past go. It came down to, "Do I want to be right in being justified in my feelings or do I want to be happy?"

As I reflected about it later, I saw that I hadn't realized how harboring my anger had been affecting my life, until I was finally able to "let it go." As soon as I did, I began discovering I had a new lease on life.

It had taken me years to get to that point when I was able to sit down with my father and have that conversation. But, I knew forgiving him was essential to my transformational process, to my moving towards my goals and having the possibility of a successful relationship. Looking back at it, now, I forgave him for *my* sake, and in return, I helped my father heal, as well.

Giving Isn't Giving, if You EXPECT Something in Return

From a young age, we begin to learn there isn't enough time, money, love, attention, energy, and in some cases, food, to go around in this world. For example, have you ever paid attention to what happens in grocery stores when the local weather forecaster announces a *huge* snowstorm, hurricane or some other weather-related drama is expected? People rush out of their homes in a frenzy to stock their kitchen with bread, milk and canned goods, remembering also to buy plenty of toilet paper and laundry soap (which will undoubtedly last for weeks)—afraid they might run out! Or better yet, remember playing "musical chairs" as a child? At the beginning of the game, everyone had a chair. Then, one by one, chairs were eliminated and the one who was left standing was "out." The basis of the game is this: *there isn't enough to go around*. I'm not saying it's the kindergarten teacher's fault, but our learned behavior begins in those types of situations.

As we grow up, we're greatly influenced by our parents, teachers, family and friends, and it is inevitable we will be predisposed to the survival skills they model, i.e., the ones that were passed down to them. Their learned skill set persuades them to operate from either crisis mode or- . . . well, I don't know many parents who demonstrate they're optimistic about a multitude of opportunities and show the courage to pursue their dreams, remaining focused, inspired and thriving. Your in-home training and all the reinforcements handed down from the various "local" influences—educational and religious institutions, cultural and economic forces, for example—will mold your individual belief system and carry an underlying power, capable of shaping, in some measure, who you become. You'll either find the world being your "oyster" (if you're not leashed to mediocre or self-sabotaging beliefs) *or* your fear-based beliefs will stifle your motivation to live a life that's authentically yours, wherein you identify your true desires and fulfill them all.

This is why it is so important to believe and know that we each have an unlimited potential and a limitless supply of resources to help fulfill our dreams . . .

and it *all* comes from Spirit, our divine source. What I've learned is that Spirit makes this available to us all, but it shows up in a variety of forms of abundance—by means of creativity, talent, good health, developed sensitivities, money, and/or "connected" people. If we *first* look to meet our supply needs in other people or in outside resources, we'll necessarily find there is a finite amount of energy resources available; but even according to physics, *the Universe is virtually unlimited*. I believe that trusting in the same power which created this magnificent Universe, us included, will never let us down. Spirit will *always* provide. Our job is to simply do our part and allow the magic to happen.

The law of "deliberate creating" is known as a universal law, which states what we focus on is what we will attract. This "law of attraction" can be found in the teachings of Abraham, which I discovered through studying the books and audio material of Ester and Jerry Hicks. In time, I applied these teachings to my life, and with relatively immediate success for example, more conscious manifesting of my desires. It should be noted here, I'm all about bending the rules, when it comes to playing the game of life; but I'm no longer tempted to break the law, when it comes to creating my destiny. Although the ideal picture you may have had in mind for your life might not appear exactly how you thought it would, it may end up being *even better* than you thought possible.

My experience has shown me that liberating oneself by "thinking outside the box" will permit the Universe's "magic" to happen, i.e., all that the Universe has in store to enrich and enhance your life. Another useful step one can take "to help the Universe help you" is to consciously acknowledge the thoughts you choose to "feed" your spirit (that is, choose wisely which to give attention to) and similarly, the energy and intentions you choose to "act on." From a more conscious space of responsible choosing, you can find the perfect opportunity to take a step back and listen to any message Spirit is offering you, especially if you are struggling in an area of your life. This process will show you "why" you are living the life you have consciously or unconsciously designed. I would add that it's never good to underestimate the value of taking time and using energy to "work" on yourself, so as to clear out any old, no-longer-useful perceptions and beliefs, as well as to simply release any past experiences that ought to be left in the past.

Giving to others, I've come to realize, is only part of the equation. Knowing how to receive completes the cycle. Receiving allows the person who is giving to "earn their wings" and feel good about themselves. When you genuinely give something away, you have no attachment to the outcome. Therefore, you expect nothing in return and there are no strings attached.

Chances are, when you give *and* expect something in return, you'll be let down, anyhow . . . because you may not get the response you were looking for.

I thought I had the "giving" lesson down, until I attracted a situation to prove to me I had some more work to do on myself. That is, I received a lesson in how to give and expect nothing in return. Interestingly, it took an encounter with a homeless man in the neighborhood to do it.

Every day, for months, I continued to see this same homeless man walking up and down the street, always minding his own business and never looking for a handout.

Because of the living situations I've found myself in more than once, I have an extra amount of compassion for anyone in need of a home. Granted, I didn't have to live on the street; but I've slept on many different sofas over the course of my life. Anyway, close to my house is a natural foods grocery store, where I spend much of my time and money. During one cold and snowy afternoon in December, I was sitting in a booth, eating my lunch, and suddenly noticed the homeless man walking by. I wanted to do something nice for him and I thought he certainly must be hungry--maybe he'd want a piece of pizza! So, I bought him two slices: one pepperoni and one cheese. But by the time I made it through the checkout counter and outside the door, he was out of my sight . . . but I was determined to find him. I jumped into my car and drove around the block. There he was, standing on the sidewalk, looking in a trash can. I parked slightly in front of him, got out of my car and approached him with the pizza. It was hard for me to control the smile on my face—I was so excited about doing a "good deed." As I got within arm's length of him, I said, "Here you go, I bought you two pieces of pizza." He looked at me, shook his head no, and said he didn't want it. I thought to myself, *What! You don't want it! You ungrateful son-of-a-gun!*

Without any hesitation, he turned around and started walking the other direction, without taking the pizza.

What a lesson he was teaching me—although, at the time, I didn't even know it—*how to give to someone and be detached about the outcome.* In this situation, I was giving with an expectation, i.e., that he wanted some pizza and would be grateful for it. My feelings were terribly hurt, because I expected a desired outcome; specifically, that he'd behave a certain way—grateful towards me!

Well, my karmic/spiritual lesson in giving without an expectation *still* wasn't complete. The Universe eventually provided me with another opportunity to give to the *same* homeless man. But this time, I was conscious about "why I was giving" and, thankfully, I wasn't expecting anything in return.

Weeks later, on *another* cold and snowy day, I was at the same market, standing at the coffee bar. Here he came, my favorite homeless guy, walking up next to me. I stopped him and asked if he wanted a cup of coffee. He looked at me and nodded his head, "Yes." When the barista handed him the fresh brewed cup of coffee, he took it from her, and just turned around and walked off. He didn't look at me, or shake my hand . . . nothing! Not even a "thank you." But it didn't matter, this time, because I wasn't expecting it *and* I was giving because I wanted to. I was excited about the fact the Universe had provided me another opportunity to give to him *and* to receive a different response.

As it so happened, the homeless fellow was standing outside as I was leaving the market. He looked directly at me with an empty heart and stoic eyes, and calmly threw his full cup of coffee away! I smiled at him and he reacted with a snub of his shoulder and a smile on his face. I think he was amused that his chucking the coffee didn't even bother me.

I might even offer to buy him another cup of coffee someday, just to keep reminding me of this concept about giving *freely* when I give.

Part 3

The Physical Lessons

Choose wisely, since you "GET" what you focus on.

You get exactly what you're looking for. That's what I've come to believe, at least. If you are seeking a relationship, a career, a dream house or . . . so many things at once that you're actually asking for a life of chaos, you will manifest exactly what your focus is on—whether it brings you happiness or not. Furthermore, what you believe about yourself *directly influences* what (or who) you will attract into your life, in order to reinforce the belief system you hold about yourself.

I began unconsciously creating my life with the "things" I was focusing on at a young age. I think this became significant, for me, in fourth grade, when I started telling my friends that, someday, I was going to marry a baseball player. And I did—at 24 years old, I married a professional baseball player. My marriage lasted six years, until we decided to part ways. Regardless of how "successful" that marriage was (or not), the reality eventually dawned on me: *you can manifest at any age.*

Once I was back in the dating game after my divorce, I wondered what it would be like to date a doctor. The Universe provided me with three opportunities—a brain surgeon, a podiatrist, and a chiropractor—all of which were great experiences, in which I learned a lot and had fun; but they didn't last, either. By then, however, I was becoming aware of the power behind manifesting. Since that time, I've been able to create wonderful opportunities, trips, cars, and dinners, without putting too much effort into it. But, *all* of these experiences were fine and dandy, until the day I woke up to the realization, that again, I was seeking happiness *outside of myself*. I had become a master at manifesting material possessions, but couldn't seem to pull it together when it came to creating a peaceful, joyful, or happy life. But through the gift of Spirit and learning by trial and error, I had an epiphany: my ideal life could only be achieved through self-mastery of the mind and learning to become patient, compassionate and vulnerable. This realization softened (somewhat) the bumps I'd been experiencing on my occasionally quite uncomfortable quest for happiness.

Without question, vision boards, God boxes, and positive affirmations are amazing tools, when it comes to assisting the conscious mind in its movement towards the direction of your desires to be, do or have. And yes, these tools do work—right up until the point where they don't! Creating your dream on paper is important, but sustainable success has to be mastered through the mind, and not allowing the emotions of fear, anger, insecurity and doubt to undermine your value as a spiritual being or invade your energy field on the spiritual, emotional or physical level.

What I can say is this: my *entire* journey has been about my ability to "know" happiness, which is an essential element in making life worth living, recognizing most of our lessons revolve around self-love. By harnessing and utilizing the conscious effort needed for connecting the dots between your experiences, you can then "own" your patterns and choose to replace them . . . consistently! This can provide you with the breakthrough in your life you've been looking for, as far as halting any repetitive or downward spiral you've been experiencing. Be aware, though: replacing thoughts, perceptions and patterns tends to be challenging and often isn't accomplished overnight, since overriding them has to be done with the same magnitude of energy or stronger than the influence needed to create it to begin with; *and* in some instances, it may be necessary to seek the help of a trained medical professional or holistic practitioner, someone to assist you in your healing process.

In my experience, I have found professionals—such as life coaches, spiritual teachers, hypnotherapists, and certified NLP or biofeedback experts—to be beneficial in attaining the emotional freedom I experience today. Feeling self-empowered emanates from having the ability to choose how you are going to respond, rather than reacting out of fear or a past irrational belief or behavior pattern. I've realized you have to keep your mind focused and your heart passionately set on what you want to achieve, and eliminate from your radar anything or anyone that doesn't support you in pursuing your dreams. These techniques have worked amazingly well for me. Put simply, I recognize *I* am the one responsible for my life, instead of consciously or unconsciously pawning that responsibility off onto someone else.

As I said, sometimes I "get" the point, and other times I discover my understanding was only temporary. There came a time when I *knew* I was clearly not getting the lessons the Universe had intended for me . . . and the stakes just went up.

Once again, the wise old saying comes to mind: "Be careful what you ask for, because you just might get it." In this instance, I wasn't paying attention to the words that were flying out of my mouth. This was a time when I had been living on a 40-acre ranch in Denver, with all of the amenities to make me look "good." To any outside observer, I'm sure I appeared quite happy. However, I had realized I was actually miserable, and those "things" were only keeping me busy making payments, cleaning, organizing, and shuffling stuff from room to room. I wasn't really happy at all! To me, it was obvious, and I also noticed I was perpetually running fast . . . but seemingly to get nowhere!

In one of my mindless states, I began to think out loud and said, "Hmm, I wonder if homeless people are happy." Since it is no secret that homeless people don't have homes, and probably don't tote big household items around in their backpacks, I wondered what it would be like to be homeless, and whether or not I could be happy being homeless. This was one of the more careless questions I could have ever asked of the Universe. However, like I said before, words carry energy and they can (and sometimes *will*) become your "thang."

The Quest for Happiness

For as far back as I can remember, I wanted to experience what it would be like to live like a "millionaire." The idea of walking into a 10,000 square foot mansion, sitting next to the pool, having the option of deciding whether or not to play tennis, golf, or basketball (in the backyard), enjoy a cigar in the cigar room, sit outside enjoying the theatre system, or choose my wine from the cellar, *all* of it sounded very appealing to me.

When this desire arose, I was sharing a house with my boyfriend. The days of my life had seemed like they were flying by. I didn't feel as though I was accomplishing any goals, and my life had been in a constant struggle—all of which made me very unhappy! I'd begun pondering the meaning of happiness, and what I needed for me to be happy. It didn't make any sense. I had the material possessions, a boyfriend, a job, and lots of friends; but something was missing. I felt "empty" on the inside. I also had the perception that everyone else was happy, but me. Then, I started thinking: *I wonder if homeless people are happy?* I wanted to find out!

I made it my "mission" to interview homeless people, so as to find out what "happiness" meant to them. Soon, I found my way to volunteering at the homeless shelter. My idea was to sit down with them during dinner, and ask them probing questions, such as: "Where do you find happiness?" and "How much effort do you put into finding happiness?" After all, if they were happy and I wasn't, what were they doing that I was missing out on?

On my first day of volunteering, I could barely contain my excitement. My volunteer jobs, at first, were serving food and using the "clicker" to count the number of people coming through the line. In between the two jobs, I was able to mingle with the few homeless people who trusted me enough to tell me something about their life stories. The majority of these had very interesting stories—so much so, I was inspired to go back the following week. The next time I came back, I found more of the same; and I was committed to going back for a third time. Strangely enough, though, I discovered I didn't have to go back for the third time

. . . because I had officially *become* one of them—yep, homeless! Since my boyfriend and I had just broken up, and I'd determined it was best for me to move out, I had been given the opportunity I wanted, alright . . . to, first hand, discover where happiness lies for homeless people.

Within a couple of days, I had moved out and begun a new chapter in my life—the quest for happiness! But, I had no idea of where that was going to lead me.

At the beginning of this adventure, I moved in with some friends who reminded me of what it must be like to live with one's grandparents. They were 80 years old and had always said, if I needed a place to "hang my hat," I would be welcome in their home. Well, one week with them ended up becoming three months. Then, it was time for me to move again. I was starting to get the "hang" of the "couch surfing/homeless" thing. This time, I lived with another set of friends and their children. I was remembering a previous lesson, and how I used to say, "I will never be homeless" or "That will never happen to me." It was my karma coming back, and a lesson in being humbled. As the saying goes, "Never say never!" and EVERYTHING I said would never happen to me, did!

There is a neighborhood in my area that has a lot of homes just like the ones I said I wanted to live in. Each day, on my way to work, I would drive through this community and say, "I'm going to live over 'there' someday." But I only had one problem. The income I was making as a massage therapist wouldn't support the dream house I desired to live in. But I remained optimistic.

Now, I thought, *it's time for me to put my manifesting skills to work.* I set an intention to make extra money and house-sit. Guess where I got to live? In the same neighborhood, with the same houses I'd said I wanted to experience, *the million dollar ones!*

The Universe was listening to me, and I had the opportunity to live in some dream homes . . . but it didn't come exactly how I thought it would. Not only was it awesome to experience living in these luxury homes, but I wasn't the one paying the bills! I was given the opportunity to enjoy wealthy people's homes, and take care of their animals, *while* getting paid to do so. It doesn't get much better than that, if you ask me. The bottom line? This sort of "manifesting" helped me fulfill one of my dreams and make it come true.

Not only was this "homeless house-sitting" a lesson in manifesting and creating the life you want to live—it was much deeper than that. It was about "me" finding happiness. I discovered through living in many different homes, big or small, rich or poor, wherever you go, there you are! You take yourself and all of your emotional baggage with you. And, if you *are* looking for happiness, you have to start with yourself. If you are not happy on the inside, there isn't a place in the world where you can buy it.

I must say, though, living the life of luxury was a blast! But it does take time, money and effort to keep it all running. It isn't all true, that money can buy you lasting happiness; because it's only temporary. "True" happiness comes from living consciously, with integrity and compassion, and being YOU!

Make Choices That Are in Alignment With Who You Are

If the choices you are making in life are not in alignment with who you are, you will struggle "from the get-go," until ultimately and unconsciously, you'll sabotage the end result. Whether or not it seems like an ideal situation, or this or that way of living or choosing seems to be working for others, it doesn't necessarily mean it will work for you. For there to really be a match, a perfect fit, it has to be congruent with who *you* are, an integral part of *your* path, and in *your* highest and best good.

It is ironic how you can "do your best," and try to make "it" work, but come up empty handed each time. This is a clear indication that the path you are on may not be the one for you, and you need to choose a different route to get to your desired goal. And sometimes, the goal you are shooting for isn't the one for you anymore. Such are the times when it's wise to use your intuition and pay attention to the "clues" the Universe is providing you, in order to help you find alignment with your purpose in life.

For example, it didn't matter how hard I tried or how many science or math classes I took, it was very clear to me that having a career as an accountant, a chemist or an architect was not part of my life's plan. Sure, I could pass the school exams, if I went to class and studied really hard; but it wasn't for me. And the harder I tried, the more frustrated I became. It was as though I was trying to put the proverbial square peg into a round hole, and it just wasn't going to work! Eventually, I could probably make the hole big enough, but a lot of swearing and suffering was bound to take place. The key, I found, is to get into the "flow" of your life, and be in alignment with who you are. With the image in your mind, acting "as-if" it has already happened, and then listening to how your body is reacting to your thought is your sign. If you begin to feel an immense amount of joy and excitement seems to be bursting from the seams within you, you are likely to be in alignment with your highest good and on the right track. But if you notice your body feels anxious, your heart begins to pound in a sporadic way, or your eyes become heavy and you feel tired at two in the afternoon, this is a good indication you should probably re-think your decision . . . *because your body is not in alignment with your decision.*

Trusting in both myself and the essential goodness of the Universe, listening to my intuition and constantly checking in with my body are now my way of life. For example, about a year ago, I was contemplating whether or not I should move to Austin, Texas. I had the perfect career opportunity, I was in a fulfilling relationship, and I had consciously created a house with the details I truly desired: beautiful hardwood floors, French doors off of the master suite, and a pool in the backyard. But somehow, it didn't feel right. I felt the pain of a two-by-four hitting me over the head when I thought about starting over again in Texas at this time in my life. My life was on hold in Denver, until Spirit gave me further instruction on where to go. Because I have felt this way in the past, but chose to not listen (at that time), I'd ended up making the "wrong" choice and suffering the consequences. This time, I intuitively knew better than to make this leap to Austin, and recognized I didn't need a "justifiable reason" to hold off on doing so. I simply continued to honor the messages my body was giving and walked away, even though my mind kept thinking I had just denied myself of a new opportunity to start all over again. But I soon saw this was *only the beginning* of a new life for me. By listening to my inner wisdom, I chose to make the best of my living situation and use this time to sit down and begin writing this book and stay in alignment with my purpose, being okay without knowing the end result.

My "Growing" Experience

A couple of years ago, when growing marijuana became "legal" (for those with specific medical needs) in Colorado, I saw the potential for me to make some fast money. Even though I had never smoked it and didn't know much about it, and thought only "losers" did this kind of thing, I decided I was going to increase my income (dramatically, I hoped) by growing it. And, to make myself feel better about the situation, I convinced myself I was doing it for medicinal purposes and helping those out who needed it.

Because I'd been a bartender for many years, I already had friends in the "growing" business. They knew how to grow, smoke, and distribute it, so I asked them for their help. At first, they were reluctant about helping me, because they knew how I felt about marijuana; but I channeled an extra dose of charm their way and convinced them to do it anyway.

To get the process started, I had to get my Medical Marijuana card. By far, this was the easiest part of the process. I made a doctor's appointment, complained of a sore arm, and they gave me my license, right on the spot.

The next step was to buy my equipment, which consisted of a seventy-five gallon reservoir, some containers, hoses, lights, and the nutrients—just like that, I was ready to begin! I hadn't a clue what I was doing, but the key, so often, is to know people who do.

Soon, the "clones" were planted, and I just needed to be patient and let the plants do what they do best—grow! I had read somewhere that if you talked to your plants or played music for them, they would grow faster and bigger. So, I tried it all. I have to admit, growing marijuana was one of the most relaxing undertakings I have ever done. Every day, it was like going to the beach. The room was humid, the breeze (or fans) were blowing, and it was hot! The only thing I was missing was the umbrella and the pina colada.

One day, the crop had finally finished growing. Within a short time, I'd harvested the goods and they were out to market. Wow!! On my first venture into the "growing business," I made a great return on my investment: $6,000 dollars! As I'd seen how well my crop was coming along, I'd already concocted a plan for the money. As soon as I got paid, I invested the $6,000 into the stock market, and I was confident I was going to double my earnings. Well, it turned out that wasn't such a good idea. In fact, it was a horrible idea! I had put all of my profits into a penny stock—which I thought for sure was "going to the moon"—until the price dropped below a penny (who knew that was even possible), and within days, my investment was gone.

Okay, okay. Just one more time, I thought (sounds familiar, right?) Yes, I felt compelled to make my money back, and *then* I was going to get out of the business.

I began the new crop just like the previous one, although it wasn't thriving like the other. But now, it didn't matter—it wasn't fun to me anymore, and I was doing it for the money, anyway. I kept at the routine maintenance I'd learned in the first "go around," and figured I'd get out of this crop whatever it yielded.

Towards the end of the growing season, I had one more "flush" to do on the plants—to clean their "systems." It was one of those days when I was in a hurry, and definitely not focused on the project at hand. (Note to self: *when you are not focused, you are likely to forget major details.*) The process of correctly doing a water change involves unplugging the pumps, draining the water out of the 75 gallon reservoir, and remembering to put everything back together. Well, I'm not a detail person, and some of the steps of the process, that day, seemed *so* time-consuming.

Around 3 a.m. that night, I was lying in bed, staring at the ceiling, when all of a sudden I heard a strange sound coming from the basement. *Oh God!* What have I done?! In a split second, I knew . . . I had forgotten to plug the pump back in!

I jumped out of bed, ran down the stairs, and watched my life flash before my eyes, just as I stepped into two inches of water that was covering the brand new bamboo floor we had just laid, *My boyfriend is going to kill me*, I shrieked to myself. We had just finished remodeling the basement, and here I was flooding it! I don't think he spoke to me for about a week after that. The cost of replacing the damaged floors and walls? About $5,000 dollars, the exact amount I was paid for the crop.

Looking back at this story, over the years, has been very interesting. In both cases, I ended up "losing" the money I had made from the "growing" experience. At the core of my being and from the beginning of this process, I *wasn't* okay with the "growing" business, and I was only doing it for the money. The Universe didn't care if I had lost my time and effort, or that I had to spend countless hours cleaning up an ocean of water that was sitting on my basement floor. I was not in alignment with who I am, and obviously, the Universe was going to see to it I was not going to benefit from something I'm not in alignment with. Ah, yes, another "growing" pain (pun intended).

Help! I Need a Sign!

Many of my most enlightening experiences have presented themselves in the form of personal relationships. In the past, I have found it extremely difficult to balance love, emotions, money and health while "standing in my truth;" therefore, several of my relationships were forced to come to an end. In each, I had found it challenging to stay in the relationship and be congruent with "who I am."

It took time and numerous heartbreaks to discover the qualities I was looking for in a partner . . . *and* what my spirit needed to be happy. But through trial and error, and maintaining my integrity, I'm now confident about expressing what is important to me in a relationship. Having my spiritual, emotional and physical needs met is essential for my happiness. I hold myself to high standards, now, and I intend for anyone I share my life with to hold themselves to similar ones. Acknowledging my "core values" and following through with my goals hasn't been easy. I have encountered emotional resistance from others, as well as from myself; but at the end of the day, I need to be able to look at myself in the mirror and be happy with the person who is staring back at me.

There *is* a particular relationship I can honestly say I learned the most from. Do you know, the one where you bang your head against the wall and ask why? It was that one! I cried every day during it. I was forced to heal childhood dramas and change my behavior and patterns that were no longer serving me. But when the day came for me to walk away from that relationship, I could do it with my head held high. I left being a better person.

There wasn't a particular incident that influenced this relationship coming to an end. It was a conglomeration of all the "little" things that slowly took away from "me." It's amazing how we ask for a sign from the Universe, to give us the "thumbs up or the thumbs down," but then we disregard the answer the Universe gives. We ask again for another sign, because the first one wasn't loud enough; and gradually the message *does* become clear . . . but also, the end of the relationship is more difficult to recover from.

Spirit gives us signs all the time; we just have to listen and pay attention. It begins with a gentle nudge, then a bump to the knee, then a baseball bat to the shoulder, and finally you get a "meteor" that has just landed on your head! Here it is! Does the Universe have your attention now? If not, then back on the hamster wheel you'll go . . . and yes, it is *all* part of your learning process.

I heard a quote: "We train people how to treat us." Yes, we do! If we don't have boundaries set up for ourselves, and don't keep ourselves accountable for our actions, chances are, others won't respect us, either. And in relationships, it is easy to lose yourself, put your needs on the back burner to accommodate other people's lives. But if the life you are living isn't feeding your Spirit, and you have lost your identity, your opinion and your dreams, true happiness does not and will not exist for you.

My Meteor!

Before Brian and I moved in together, things were great between the two of us. Then we bought a house together and everything changed. Our lifestyles weren't as similar as we once had thought, and I began to feel resentful, angry and just didn't care about the direction my life was headed. I lost interest in my health, the way I was "presenting" myself in the world, and I had lost hope that the world is an abundant place in which to live. Down deep, I knew the relationship was coming to an end, but didn't have the guts to get out, and would, on a daily basis, find enough reasons for me stay. *I'm just going to deal with it,* I thought to myself. Well, I wasn't good at JUST dealing with it, and it was only a matter of time before I'd "go into orbit!"

I needed a change, but didn't know "how" or "what" to do. But, as it worked out, I didn't have to find a solution—Spirit did it for me. However, I *did* ask for a sign, and I was very specific. I prayed, "I need a sign for me to let me know if I am supposed to stay in this relationship or not, so please give me a meteor . . . and make it obvious."

That weekend, Brian and I decided to go camping. I didn't want to go, but I wanted to keep the peace, so I chose to go anyway. Every part of my being was telling me not to go, but I apparently like to learn my lessons the hard way.

It was the first weekend of the camping season and it was cold outside. We drove halfway to our destination, and then pulled over to make dinner and sleep for the night. As we were getting ready for bed, Brian put his loaded handgun on a shelf, above the window. I crawled over to my side, reached behind me to turn the light off, and my hand accidently bumped the handgun. I knocked it off of the ledge, and it hit me in the side of the head. BAM! It went off! Luckily, neither of us were hit by a bullet . . . however, was *that* a sign or what? I *did* ask for a meteor, didn't I? I guess I had to get hit in the head with a loaded handgun to really "pay attention" to what I was allowing into my life.

So, I lay there, very still, and could see blood spewing out from the side of my head. I wiggled my fingers and toes, to make sure they were still there. I felt for my front teeth, to make sure they were still there. Okay, life was good: I still had all my body parts and I was still alive. *Seriously!* I said to myself. Although, I did ask for an obvious sign, did it almost have to kill me? But, reflecting back on my relationship with Brian and how I was living my life, I had *not* been standing in my truth. In fact, everyday, I felt like a part of me had been dying.

Certainly, our intention is to attract relationships into our lives to experience love, so we can love others, and to love ourselves enough to be honest with who we are and challenge ourselves to stay on our path. What I've found is that you have to live your life according to your purpose, with the passions that inspire you, and live the life that supports who you are. Without a doubt, changing any situation in life is challenging. When fear arises, there may come a point when it can be unbearable to "stay where you are." But if you don't make the change, the consequences can be far worse. I recall that old saying about "saving your face, but losing your soul."

The great thing about this experience is this: I only have a "little" scar on my eyebrow from where I was hit with the gun, *but* it is my constant reminder to stay on track and in alignment with who I am.

Living on the Edge

How do you know when you are on the right path? Have faith and listen to your "gut" or inner wisdom. It is given to you for a reason. Answers in life are seldom black and white. More often, it seems there are many shades of gray, many "layers" of truth. Sometimes, doors will close, but they'll end up being seen to have done so *in your favor* . . . so another *better* one can open. But how do you know when to change course? There have been a number of instances along my path when I thought, "This is it! This is the perfect relationship" or "I have finally found my life's calling." Then, however, "reality" shows up, my dreams are shattered, and I have to pick up the pieces and start all over again. Letting go and giving up have two different meanings.

There is a different energy around "letting go." When you willingly set something free, you detach from the outcome and allow the Universe to work its magic, bringing it back to you, if it was meant to be. If you give up, on the other hand, there typically is anger and resentment attached to the "giving up." This observation reinforces the lesson of detachment, the releasing of any "need to control" . . . and a simple trusting that the Universe has another plan for you—a better one! The best thing you can do, when you're at your breaking point, is surrender, ask Spirit for help, and believe the highest and best is yours to have.

Signs given to you from Spirit or from your intuition—that "gut feeling" . . . or knowing you're on the "right" track or path in life—can show up in a variety of ways: dreams, people, animals, feathers, pennies, or any object that has a significant meaning to you. For me, asking for a sign to confirm I'm moving in the right direction is normally my "M.O." (mode of operation). I also ask Spirit for a sign to let me know if the choice I'm making is in my highest and best interest, or if I am I making the best choice for future success. Since I'm typically "looking for it," getting a sign from Spirit happens to be a frequent experience for me, an everyday occurrence, actually.

Also, when I feel as though all hope is lost, I ask for a sign, to give me confirmation I'm on the right path, to keep me moving forward, or to change my course of action. Not only is receptivity to signs about listening, but also about accepting "what is," and having the courage to do something different. When I'm at a crossroads, I try to rise above the situation and approach it from being an observer, as if I am looking through "another" person's eyes. When we are in the middle of our own chaos, it is difficult to make sense of the situation and know if what we are seeing is "real" or if it is a manifestation of our own mind's "illusion" (i.e., mistaken or misguided beliefs).

I was moving into a new apartment, and although the complex was beautiful, I didn't feel "safe." So, I remedied the situation, by changing the locks, keeping the lights on, using feng shui principles to balance the house's energy, and making the home "mine," by decorating it with my "stuff." Also, my intuition was telling me I needed to find a picture of a cloud. So, I decided to go shopping.

Browsing through a number of furniture stores, I finally found what I was looking for: two 10"x20" pictures of "angelic" nature scenes—clouds and a luscious green path leading up to the sky, reminding me of what I thought "heaven" would look like if I ever made it. These pictures gave me a feeling of being "safe. "

Years flew by, and I decided to move again *and* get a roommate. But my roommate didn't find the pictures as calming as I did. He suggested, if I was going to hang them in our new place, I should get them reframed to look more contemporary. In the spirit of harmony, I agreed.

I found a framing expert in the area, and created a frame that would make us both happy. But, unforetunately, when the frames were complete, my resources were limited, and my car was in desperate need of repair, including its needing a new set of tires. I was bummed. I had no other choice, other than to fix my car, and to abandon my pictures, leaving them with the framer.

Well, three years later, I joined Toastmasters, a public speaking organization. There, I met and became new friends with a woman named Lori. She knew I was a feng shui practioner, and asked me if I would come over to her house and give her a consultation. After she had moved into her condominium, she had learned of numerous break-ins in the area, making her fearful of living in her own environment. Eventually, she asked me if I had any feng shui suggestions.

As it turned out, at that time, I was questioning my own path in life--wondering if I was still living in alignment with my purpose. It was a Sunday afternoon, and I was headed over to Lori's house. I walked in, and guess what I saw hanging on the wall? My cloud pictures! Both of them!! They had "shown up" in my life

AGAIN, but only in a different way. Even though they were no longer mine, I was so happy to see them. I yelled, "Those are my pictures!" I knew they were mine, as I had designed the frames. But to be absolutely positive, I had to ask her where she had purchased them—naturally, it was from the framer I had originally taken them to. I have to admit, it was a little weird looking at my pictures on her wall.

I reminded myself of what my intention was when I purchased them. They made me "feel" safe, and reminded me of "heaven." I can honestly say, from the moment I saw my pictures hanging on her wall, I knew neither one of us had a thing to be afraid of, that we were both on the "right" path in life. It was obvious they had appeared in Lori's life for the same reason they had originally appeared in mine . . . as a reminder that we are always guided.

Carrying on with the consultation, and having established we are both "safe" and on our "path," Lori and I were sitting in the living room, looking at the brick fireplace. I was contemplating how to "spruce it up." I came up with the suggestion to hang a mirror above the mantle. She loved the idea and had the perfect circular mirror, which was so conveniently located in her basement. We found it, dusted it off, and hung it up. It looked great!

We proceeded to tell each other about our life's stories. In the midst of mine, I made a comment to her, "I like to live my life on the edge." Just as I said the word "edge," the mirror we'd placed above the mantle came crashing down! KABOOM! We ducked down, covered our heads with our hands, and thought for sure the world was crashing down around us.

We gingerly walked over to the mirror, thinking it had to have shattered in a million little pieces . . . *but it was unbroken*. It had bypassed the mantle *and* the hearth, and was lying in the middle of the floor. We look at each in amazement! As if the cloud picture fiasco wasn't "crazy" enough, now the mirror crashes seven feet to the floor and doesn't break. WOW!

To me, the mirror was another sign: it symbolized that, even though I am living life on the edge, and I may fall, I won't break. The "message" I read into it was for me to keep moving forward.

What Goes Around, Comes Around

My mother always told me my mouth would get me into trouble, if I didn't watch it . . . and she was right. I've spoken my mind whenever and however I was moved to, and I've stuck up for those who did not have much of a voice—like the elderly, children and animals. Many nights, I've found myself sleeping on the sofa, a chair or even in my camper for insisting on proving my point or confronting someone who was treating another person or animal poorly. I just couldn't walk away or turn my head and watch someone or something being abused. I would defiantly speak my peace and then let them know "paybacks are a bitch." Nevertheless, my philosophy in life was and, to some degree, still is: I can run fast and they won't catch me! That is, given my running speed and agility, I'm not all that afraid of stating my truth to someone, if I'm the one they're going to come after next to seek their revenge. In other words, back then, especially, I didn't let anything stand in my way of expressing my thoughts. Looking back, it has taken me 35 years to learn how to put a filter on my mouth, and there are times I could still use some duct tape! It wasn't until recently that I figured out effective communication is largely about the delivery. In other words, it is not what you say, but how you say it. If you want people to listen and react to you in a positive manner, you have to speak their language. In my time, I have won a few arguments (although I've probably lost many more), but it was part of the game—the game of growing up. Acquiring the skills to effectively communicate takes time, but such skills need to be learned . . . if one cares about finding some true success, fulfillment and emotional freedom in life.

Like I mentioned, what goes around, comes around. This may have been the most valuable lesson of all time, for me. I spent the first 16 years of my life living with my mother and brother. Then, because of my mother's drinking, my brother and I moved to a foster home for a period of time, until my mother decided to seek help for her alcoholism. But up until we had moved out, it wasn't unusual for us to be sharing our home with a foster child or someone who didn't have a place to go for the holidays. For selfish reasons, I would give my mother a dirty look and ask her, "Why do THEY need to eat with us?" or "Why don't THEY have another place to go?" or "Why don't THEY have a family?" *Why?! Why?! Why?!* My mother's response was always the same: "Because you never know when *you* are going to need help someday." And, she was right. The time eventually came when I *did* need help . . . and lots of it! Words have power. When you say, "That will NEVER happen to me," you are actually challenging the Universe to teach you a lesson.

It was one of those days, when I was throwing a pity party for myself. *Poor me*, I whined to myself. *My job isn't good enough, I'm too fat, my hair isn't the right color*, and my complaints went on and on.

That afternoon, on my way home from work, I stopped in at the grocery store, to pick up dinner. And like usual, I was in a hurry. I rushed inside, grabbed my items, and scoped out the shortest line—only to stand in the one that took the longest.

Because patience has never been one of my fortes, it was typical to find myself in the slowest line and totally missing the point about how good the Universe is to me. Impatiently waiting and, of course, tapping my foot, I was so concerned with my own life, I wasn't paying attention to the people standing around me. When the checkout clerk had finished ringing up my groceries, I finally made eye contact with him, and realized he had a learning disability.

He looked at me, and smiled, “Guess what?” he said. “What?” I replied, changing the tone of my voice. “I’m going to be an astronaut, someday.” “Really?” I answered. “Yep, and guess what else I’m going to do? I’m going to go to medical school and become a doctor for the astronauts, just in case they get sick while they’re on the moon.”

I took a deep breath and said, “I think you should go for it. I bet you will be the best astronaut the world has ever seen.” He was so excited. “Do you really think so? You think I can do it?” I smiled at him and nodded. “You bet I do!”

When I left the grocery store, I said to myself, “What is my problem again?” Here I am, I have my health, a great education, a good job, a very nice car, the world by the tail, and I’m whining about not having “enough,” when in fact, I have more than enough, and I am extremely blessed!

That day, the store clerk changed my hopeless attitude, and put my life in perspective. That incident helped me realize how fortunate I really am. I *was*, indeed, capable of creating and living the life I want to live, and my “poor me” attitude wasn’t going to get me anywhere.

At the End of the Day . . .

What you make of your life is up to you. We are here to live, laugh, grow and share with others . . . and in return, our hearts, minds and souls will be reaping the benefits.

Some of you may be wondering, "How do you consider your life to be 'charmed,' based on so many not-so charming experiences, Angela?" I'd reply, it's because there isn't a doubt in my mind that I'm not alone on my journey, and I believe in the magic of the Universe. I can appreciate the value of each lesson, person, relationship, animal and situation I encounter, for what it is, realizing that as I accept it, I can love and appreciate each for their role in shaping the person I've become. Without these encounters and my experiencing Spirit in the ways I have—inclusive of my enduring hardships, ordeals and challenging relationships, *and* my having received signs along the way to inspire me to keep going—it would be impossible for me to suggest to others to keep their faith, surrender their doubts and fears, and trust that their highest good is being seen to by countless unseen, yet truly benevolent "forces."

There have been numerous times when I've been amongst a group of people, and someone will be telling a story about a "miracle" they'd experienced in their lives. And it baffles me to hear them saying they don't know who to "thank," because they're uncertain of "who" to trust in. It doesn't matter if you label the divine intervention God, Spirit, Buddha, or the Universe—just believe in something bigger than yourself and be grateful for it! Now, it is not my job to convince you to believe anything whatsoever. These are experiences Spirit has given me, and insights Spirit has shown me, which have gotten me to where I am today. We all have free choice and free will, and we can do whatever we wish. But my path *wouldn't* have been quite so graced, if I wouldn't have been "pushed" to the edge, forcing me to trust and allow Spirit to work through me.

Writing this book, for instance, has been one of the most difficult tasks I've ever done. It has taken me years of experiences and a great deal of growth in my understanding of these challenges to be able to put them down on paper. I have spent hours staring at my computer screen, not being able to type a word . . . because in my mind, I would think, *Who would want to read this, in the first place?* Ultimately, I wrote this for me. It had been a project I've wanted to do since I can remember, and now Spirit has given me the opportunity to make it a reality. Not only did I decide to write this book, but I also had the idea to manufacture a "butterfly charm" as a visual reminder to stay in alignment with my highest self and believe in endless possibilities. The reason it's in the shape of a butterfly is because it symbolizes transition, freedom, beauty and grace, many of the qualities that influence an inspired way of living.

Inevitably, there will be people on your path who will make you question your belief system, your goals, your values and yourself. That is what those people are there for—to "reflect back to you" the importance of keeping on your path and not allowing their opinion to influence you to doubt, hesitate or give up. You take what works for you, apply it to your life and leave the rest. Back in the day, I had a boyfriend who told me I laughed too much and I smiled too big! He typically followed those statements up with, "Why are you so interested in saving the world, anyway?" Needless to say, I chose to get out of that relationship in a hurry!

Never play small to accommodate someone else's insecurities. Such matters are *their* problems, not yours.

Life is about choices—and sometimes, *not* making a choice is making a choice. When evaluating who and what we expend our "energy" and attention on, it is important to ask ourselves: "Is this person or situation adding to my life *or* taking away from my life?"

And by the way, sticking your head in the sand and pretending that person or those situations don't exist won't get you anywhere, except more of what you already have.

I didn't reinvent the wheel, when it comes to changing your life and living your dreams. However, I *have* followed other people's advice and applied their recipes, for success . . . *and* I've discovered my own "formulas for fulfillment" within the process.

10 Daily Habits for a Charmed Journey

If I had to sum my "fulfilling life formula" up in 10 daily habits I regularly do (and suggest), ones that have produced the greatest results in my life, they would all proceed from the words "Strive to":

Be in a state of gratitude—Never let a day go by without being thankful for what you have . . . and don't focus on what you don't have. If you can't find anything to be grateful for, start by being thankful that you are still breathing. Finding value in every situation will continue to move you forward and closer to living the life you most deeply desire to live.

Be willing to change—Open yourself up to doing something different, encourage yourself to get out of your "comfort zone," and expand your horizons. *Noth-*

ing stays the same. You have to evolve with the world, as well as with the people in it. Albert Einstein said, "The definition of insanity is doing the same thing over and over again, expecting a different result."

Be kind—Showing kindness and compassion to people, animals and Mother Earth will bring untold blessings upon you. To keep your life in check, ask yourself, "How am I 'being' and behaving when no one else is looking?" The old proverb holds true: *What goes around, comes around*. If you want others and the world to treat you well, treat others *and life itself* kindly. The world responds to the energy you "put out."

Be goal-oriented—Setting goals and creating some sort of accountability for your progressing toward them is a great way to keep you motivated and focused. It doesn't matter what goals you set—just be sure they're clear and concrete, realistic, and in alignment with your true self! These days, going the extra mile is expected, but your willingness to go an extra *hundred* miles will help you in achieving your dream. Personal successes seldom happen overnight. When you start a project, hang in there long enough to see it through. If and when the "signs" indicate to you it is time to "let it go," be willing to detach from the venture and move on.

Be healthy—Think happy thoughts, eat healthy foods and move your body in healthy ways. "As above, so below" holds true with how our thoughts and emotions affect our bodies. Adequate protein, fruits and vegetables are essential for providing the body and mind with a proper foundation for sustaining health, growth and success. By doing so, you'll also preserve a higher vibration of energy within yourself and more well-balanced brain chemistry. Research has shown that increasing the chemical balance in a person's brain enhances one's ability to function at an optimum capacity, enabling them to respond to life's challenges with more clear and rational thinking. Here's another way to view the road to health—healthy food is preventative medicine. *Eat well and be well.* If you can't pronounce the ingredients on the label, chances are, you shouldn't be eating it. Our bodies only function as well as the "energy" we put into it. And certainly, exercise or regular physical movement (walking, hiking, swimming, dancing, whatever!) makes a huge difference in how healthy and "in shape" you are. Since we've got physical bodies, then (as Olivia Newton-John sings), "Let's get physical!"

Be of service—Serving the needs of others is a way of giving back what we ourselves have been given. The "circle of life" is completed when we give of ourselves. And, when we do something for someone else, we are also getting out of our own problems and focusing on helping others. In return, this can provide us with insights and time to reevaluate our own situation. By doing so, we can perhaps approach our own life challenges from a different perspective. How many times have you heard, "I will volunteer when I have the time." Why wait? Make time, because you may never find the time.

Be passionate—People ask me frequently, "How do you find your passion?" or they say, "I don't have a passion." Sure you do! Everyone has a passion! God wouldn't put us here without having *something* we can be passionate about! We are meant to live a happy, inspired and extraordinary life. When you are passionate about something, you feel it in your blood, it energizes you, and time flies by without you noticing. If you're not currently inspired and passionate about something in your life, it may take trying new activities, going to workshops or classes, reading books, or just being willing to take a risk about something you've felt held back to explore in the past (but always wanted to). Ultimately, you may find you have different desires than you'd previously had. That's alright, since passions can change as you evolve. The main thing is to find what it is that "floats your boat" and (as Nike's ads say) "Just do it." It's true! At any given moment, you can just decide to *do* something different, especially if you put your whole heart into making the "doing" (and your life) the best it can be.

Be charming—Engage in other people's lives and make them feel "special" for who they are. Be influential and complimentary with your words and deeds. Smile with your eyes, be genuine and real, and encourage others to live their dreams.

Be inspired—Stay connected with Spirit and be open to the "magic" that is all around you. Be willing to receive divine guidance, and trust that the highest good is working on your behalf . . . *always!*

Be you—See the beauty in who you are. Be authentic and honest about what makes you happy. No one is as committed to your life as you are. Make choices in life that feed *your* spirit and move *you* closer to *your* dreams.

In summary, live your life with purpose. There will be times when you may be forced to remove your rose-colored glasses and take a good look at yourself, to reevaluate who you are and what you have come here to do. Put your best foot forward and never lose sight of your dreams *or* your faith in achieving them. If it is in alignment with who you are and part of the Divine's plan, it will manifest . . . *right before your eyes.*

Epilogue

The Universe is continually providing for me. I don't know how the things of my life are all supposed to come together; but they seem to be doing so. For example, when I was in the market for some professional photos of myself for this book, I was out for a walk one day and a woman came up to me, mentioned she had heard I was a massage therapist, and was wondering if I would trade with her. I asked her what she did and she said she's a photographer for authors. How cool is that! *She approached me!*

This has been my life for the past couple of years . . . quite charming, really! ☺

About the Author

Angela Lenhardt earned a B.A. from the University of Northern Colorado in Business Management and Finance. She owns a healing practice in Denver, Colorado and has traveled through China and Thailand studying alternative medicine, Feng Shui, Qigong, meditation, yoga and Tai massage. Angela brings together the knowledge of many masters to support her clients in positive transformation; offering tools and encouragement to create a life full of potential and desired outcomes.

If you are interested in scheduling an intuitive coaching session or Feng Shui consultation, please contact Angela at 720-837-7568 or by email at Angela@angelalenhardt.com.

27619165R00109

Made in the USA
Charleston, SC
16 March 2014